SRI LANKA
SERENDIPITY UNDER SIEGE

What is the root of the communal violence in Sri Lanka?

The country is riven by ethnic conflict between the majority Sinhalese, who are mainly Buddhist, and the minority Tamils, who are mainly Hindu. Since 1983 the situation has deteriorated alarmingly.

This important book, based on reports prepared for LawAsia — the Association of Lawyers for Asia and the Pacific — examines the violence which increasingly affects unarmed citizens. It also considers the serious erosions of democracy and the rule of law in a country where both were formerly prized. In an epilogue, the significance of the Indo-Sri Lanka Accord, signed in response to the surge of violence in 1987, is considered.

Serendip is a former name for Sri Lanka. From it comes *serendipity*, the faculty of making happy chance finds.

Patricia Hyndman is the Honorary Secretary of the LawAsia Human Rights Committee and Associate Professor of Law at the University of New South Wales.

SRI LANKA
SERENDIPITY UNDER SIEGE

Patricia Hyndman

Spokesman

First published in 1988 by:
Spokesman
Bertrand Russell House
Gamble Street
Nottingham, England
Tel. 0602 708318

ISBN 0-85124-467 8 Hardcase
ISBN 0-85124-477 7 Paperback

Printed by the Russell Press Ltd, Nottingham
(Tel. 0602 784505)

CONTENTS

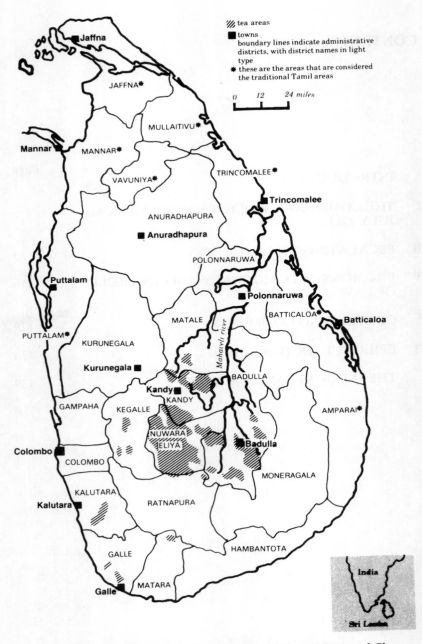

Map of Sri Lanka reproduced by kind permission of *Race and Class*
(© Institute of Race Relations, 1984.)

I

INTRODUCTION

LAWASIA (the Association of Lawyers for Asia and the Pacific) has had a close connection with Sri Lanka for some years. Sri Lankan lawyers have been among its members from the time of its formation in 1966. In 1979 the Sixth Biennial LAWASIA Conference was held in Colombo, and, for the period from 1979 to 1981, Mr. Harry Jayewardene, QC, the President's brother and close adviser, was the President of LAWASIA. It was at the 1979 Colombo conference that the Human Rights Standing Committee came into being. Many members of LAWASIA have developed friendships and close ties with lawyers, judges and other people within Sri Lanka.

In view of this background there is considerable interest and concern amongst LAWASIA members about the troubling events which have in recent years come to plague the country with both increasing frequency and increasing ferocity.

During the last week of July, 1983, a severe outbreak of communal violence in Sri Lanka saw hundreds of the minority Tamil community killed, thousands left injured and homeless, and the systematic destruction of Tamil shops, houses and factories. Tamil civilians and their property in the capital, Colombo, and in many different towns and villages, were attacked in organised acts of mob violence perpetrated by sectors of the majority community, the Sinhalese. The security forces significantly failed to provide the minority with adequate protection, and, in some cases, actively participated in the atrocities.

At that time the world was shocked that such events should have taken place in a country widely regarded as one in which the rule of law prevailed and democratic traditions were prized.

In August, 1983, expressing its concern at these occurrences, the LAWASIA Human Rights Standing Committee sought, and was granted, government permission to send a fact-finding mission to enquire into the circumstances of these disturbances. The delegates for this mission were Mr. Samiuddin Zhouand, a former judge of the Court of Appeal and former Deputy Attorney-General of Afghanistan, and Patricia Hyndman, Honorary Secretary of the LAWASIA Human Rights Committee and Associate Professor in the Faculty of Law, University of New South Wales, Sydney, Australia. After this visit a report was prepared and presented to the LAWASIA Human Rights Standing Committee, *The Communal Violence in Sri Lanka, July 1983*.

The violence generated by the ethnic conflict between the majority (74%) Sinhalese, who are mainly Buddhist, and the minority (18.2%) Tamils, who are mainly Hindu, has continued to escalate to alarming proportions. In view of this deteriorating situation within Sri Lanka, the LAWASIA Human Rights Standing Committee early in 1985 again requested, and received, government permission to send a delegate to Sri Lanka, and Patricia Hyndman was asked to return to update her earlier report. She made a 5 day visit from February 17th to 22nd, 1985.

During both missions interviews were conducted with government members and officials, members of opposition parties and the Tamil United Liberation Front (TULF), lawyers, members of bodies such as the Sri Lanka Foundation, the International Centre for Ethnic Studies, the Civil Rights Movement and the Centre for Society and Religion, groups of concerned citizens, religious groups and members of trade unions.

Both reports are based upon the information acquired from the interviews conducted while in Sri Lanka; from legal documents; press reports, both local and international; material put out by various organisations and other documentation obtained both while in the country and after leaving. The second report was finalised on June 7th, 1985.

Tragically, since that time the situation in Sri Lanka has continued on its course of violence and destruction. People from both sides, both combatants and non-combatants, are being killed, injured, dislocated from their normal way of life, and have had their property looted, damaged or totally destroyed. According to statistics from a variety of sources, between mid-July 1983 and early February 1987 more than 5,000 people have died as a direct consequence of the civil strife. Approximately 200 civilans, the majority of them Tamil, were massacred in one week in early 1987.

During the past two years the Sri Lankan government and Tamil leaders (both from the TULF party and militant groups) have made attempts at negotiation. The Indian government has, on several occasions, acted as mediator. Talks have begun, been broken off, and started again. Within both sides there have been internal conflicts about which, if any, of the proposed solutions are acceptable. Today (February 1987), agreement on the terms of a peaceful solution, and negotiated settlement, seem as far away as ever they were. Hostilities and tensions continue to increase, as, it appears, does the determination, in factions on both sides, to achieve solution by military victory. It may still be possible for dialogue between the Sinhalese and the Tamils to be established and to work, but the longer the current hostilies, violence and destruction continue, the more difficult it must inevitably become to bridge the widening gaps and the growing resentments between the two groups.

The LAWASIA observer mission reports are concerned with two inter-related phenomena; firstly, the violence which increasingly has been affecting unarmed citizens, and which continues to escalate, and, secondly, the erosions both of democracy and of the rule of law. These trends, sadly, have been pronounced in Sri Lanka in recent years. Although some time has passed since the completion of the reports the themes with which they are concerned continue to be of vital importance in Sri Lanka today. In this book the reports have been combined. They are presented in the following manner.

First, a specific outbreak of violence, that which occurred in July 1983, is reported in some detail. This section begins with an account of the ambush in Jaffna of 13 soldiers on July 23rd, and the revenge which the armed forces took on the civilian population of that region on July 24th and the days following. Next, the arrangements for the burial of the soldiers at the Kanatte Cemetery are recorded, as is the violence which began there and which then spread to other parts of Colombo and then to different centres within the country. Then the course which the violence took and the actions of the security forces are outlined. The July 25th and July 27th massacres of Tamil political prisoners in Welikade prison are documented next, then the events of Friday July 29th, "Black Friday", followed by an enumeration of some of the direct consequences of the disturbances, and a record of some specific incidents affecting individuals and their families. There follows an account of government censorship, the statements and responses to the week of disturbances made by government ministers, and the promulgation of the Sixth Amendment. Finally, some of the theories as to both the reasons behind the behaviour of the security forces and the causes of the outbreak of the disturbances are listed.

Second, the subject of escalating violence is considered. Under this heading there is, firstly, an account of the grievances perceived by the Tamil and Sinhala communities in relation to each other. Without this background it is difficult to appreciate the current situation. In this context the topics examined are: the status of Tamils of "recent Indian origin"; university education and state sector employment; the problems caused by the existence of two major languages and the status of the Tamil language; colonisation; decentralisation; the demand for 50:50; the 1948, 1972 and 1978 Constitutions; the identification of Buddhism with Sinhalese nationalism, and the minority syndrome as perceived by different groups within Sri Lankan society. After a consideration of this background, the steps taken by Tamils to secure for themselves what they see as their due measure of recognition within Sri Lanka and the rise of Tamil militancy are considered.

Next some of the measures taken by the present government in its attempts to curb both Tamil violence and the activities leading towards separatism are examined. Those outlined are: the proclamation of a state of emergency; the emergency regulations, those which establish the prohibited and security zones in the north and east and other emergency legislation; press coverage, propaganda and censorship regulations; the enactment and continuation of The Prevention of Terrorism Act; the mass arrests which have been made of young Tamil males from some areas in the north; the passage of the Sixth Amendment; the meetings of the All Party Conference and its collapse at the end of 1984, and government action on earlier recommendations. Also outlined are the reprisal attacks which have been made upon the civilian population of the north and east by members of the security forces. Government actions indicating a commitment to human rights principles and a willingness to improve relationships with the Tamil people are examined, as well as positive indications of a desire amongst ordinary citizens to build bridges of understanding and dialogue between the communities.

Turning to the third topic, that of erosions of democracy and the rule of law, the items covered here are: the 1978 Constitution and the powers which it confers upon the President; amendments to that Constitution; new legislation concerning conduct at elections; the proscription of opposition parties; threats to the independence of the judiciary, and incidents tending to encourage lawlessness.

II

THE COMMUNAL VIOLENCE IN SRI LANKA, JULY 1983

i) Introduction to the first LAWASIA report, February 1984.
The LAWASIA Human Rights Standing Committee sent a delegation
to Sri Lanka from August 25 — September 1 1983, as a fact finding
mission to enquire into the circumstances of the outbreak of communal
violence which occurred in that country during the last week of July
1983, and to consider these occurrences against LAWASIA's Ten Basic
Principles of Human Rights. At the end of that period this report was
prepared by Patricia Hyndman and presented to the LAWASIA Human
Rights Standing Committee.

While in Sri Lanka the delegation received very full co-operation from
all quarters and was able to interview the following people: His
Excellency, President Jayewardene; government officials, including
Mr. B. Weerakoon, Commissioner General of Essential Services; Mr.
D. Liyanage, Secretary, Ministry of State and the Competent Authority
for Publications; General D. S. Atygalla, Secretary, Ministry of
Defence; Mr. Weerapittia, Deputy Minister of Defence; Mr. M.
Wijesinghe, Secretary, Ministry of Justice; Mr. W.T. Jayasinghe,
Secretary, Ministry of Foreign Affairs; Mr. Nesiah, Government Agent
in Jaffna; and Commander A. Perera, Chairman, REPIA
(Rehabilitation of Property and Industrial Authority); some military
personnel; members of some opposition parties, including Mr.
Amirthalingam, leader of the TULF party; several other TULF
members of parliament; and Mrs. Bandaranaike, former leader of the
SLFP; some university staff and students; trade union officials, including
Mr. S. Thondaman, leader of the Ceylon Workers Congress (CWC);
lawyers, (in addition some Sri Lankan lawyers, including Mr. H.W.
Jayewardene, QC, the President's brother and close adviser, and Mr.
K.S. Wijawardena, Chief Magistrate for Colombo, were interviewed
one week later by Patricia Hyndman at the time of the 8th Biennial
LAWASIA conference held in Manila); members of civil rights groups;
community and religious organisations; a cross-section of members of
the Tamil minority groups; some of the families affected by the violence,
and some of the displaced persons at two displaced persons' camps.

Many of the people interviewed have not been named in the report.
Some have not been named in connection with specific information to
ensure that they will not be in any way adversely affected by the help
that they provided. Although the sources are not always identified, care

was taken throughout to ensure that, as far as possible, all shades of opinion were canvassed. An exception was that no contact at all was made with any of the militant groups.

The government both facilitated meetings with its members, and gave very much appreciated assistance with transport and general contacts. The co-operation extended by the government was of very great assistance to the delegation, releasing as it did time for further interviews which otherwise would have been occupied by the making of necessary travel and other organisational arrangements.

The delegation pursued its own contacts among members of the opposition parties and other groups, and particularly as regards the communications made with Tamil people.

The information contained in the report and the conclusions drawn in it are based mainly upon information obtained at interviews, and upon observations which the delegation was able to make while in Sri Lanka. The report was finalised on February 7, 1984. It was not possible at that time to update all of it. Those parts upon which further information was available were updated as far as was possible. For much of the report, however, the only reliable information available was that collected at the time of the delegation's visit to Sri Lanka. Accordingly most of the report is based on this material.

The factual account of the occurrences of the week of communal disturbances at the end of July 1983 is based upon information provided either by eye-witnesses to events, or, where no eye-witnesses came forward, from reliable sources whose information received ample corroboration from others.

An assessment, of course, had to be made as to the reliability and impartiality of these sources of information. Statements were not accepted at face value; questions were asked, corroboration was sought, and several different sources and perspectives were sought out and obtained on most matters. Checks were made against legal documents, press reports both local and international, government publications, material put out by various organisations, and other documentation obtained both whilst in Sri Lanka and after leaving.

It is appreciated that mistakes and distortions may nevertheless occur. Every effort has been made to eliminate errors, and the information given below is believed to be accurate.

The delegation spent 6 days in Colombo and 1 day in Jaffna. The opportunity to spend 1 day in Jaffna was made possible by the government's provision of transportation by air-force plane. The facilities made available and the overwhelming courtesy, co-operation and assistance received from government members, and from all persons met by the delegation, are recorded here with sincere appreciation. Special thanks are made to Mr. E.A.G. de Silva, the Sri Lankan member to the LAWASIA Human Rights Standing Committee, for his unfailing kindness, help, care and thoughtfulness throughout the week.

A. Factual account of the communal violence, July 1983.

i) Introduction

Saturday, July 23rd 1983, marks the beginning of a week of violence in Sri Lanka that shook the nation, and indeed the entire world. Sri Lanka is widely regarded as a country which has an excellent reputation for upholding democratic principles, respecting human rights and in which the rule of law prevails, so that the fierce outbreak of communal violence against a minority group which took place at that time was all the more shocking for these reasons.

The violence was directed against the Tamil population of the country. Hundreds were killed, thousands were displaced from their usual places of residence, very many of them losing everything they owned. There was great property damage and scars were inflicted which will take time and concentrated effort to heal.

In Sri Lanka the population is predominantly Sinhalese, these people comprise 74% of all the people in the country. Just over 7% of the population is made up of Muslims, and 0.7% were described as "Others" in the 1981 census figures. Tamils form 18.2% of the population, of these 12.6% are Sri Lankan Tamils who have been in the country for many hundreds of years, and 5.6% are Indian Tamils, who were brought over from India by the British during the last century to work on the plantations as indentured labour.

It is important to note that, while these figures show the overall composition of the Sri Lankan population, Tamils (Sri Lankan and Indian) form 97.7% of the population in the district of Jaffna, 89.9% in that of Mullaitivu, 76.3% in Vavuniya, 72% in Batticoloa, 64.0% in Mannar, and 36.4% in Trincomalee, (1981 census figures). In order to reach a true appreciation of the country's ethnic problems both these sets of figures have to be borne in mind. Ethnic minorities distributed uniformly throughout a population tend not to develop the same group identity, nor to experience the same difficulties, as do those minorities which live in concentrated bodies in particular regions.

ii) The ambush of July 23rd

The Jaffna peninsula, which is at the northern-most tip of the island, is the region of Sri Lanka with the greatest percentage of Tamils in its population. The 1981 census shows that 97.7% of its inhabitants are Tamil people, 95.3% being Sri Lankan Tamils and 2.4% Indian Tamils.

In Jaffna late in the evening of Saturday, July 23rd, 13 soldiers were killed in an ambush. Those interviewed had no doubt that this was the work of Tamil militants. Several militant groups, comprised of disaffected Tamil youth, have been operating in the north since the mid-1970s. They wish to secure a separate state, which they call Eelam, within Sri Lanka for the Tamil people, and they see violence as the only means by which to redress Tamil grievances.

The targets of the militants have been military personnel or police stationed in the north, those who inform the authorities against them, and moderate Tamil politicians who are seen as co-operating with the present government. Many Tamil people have been attacked or killed by the militants, but, on this occasion, the 13 soliers killed in the ambush were all Sinhalese. Since the composition of the army is predominantly Sinhalese, it is of course likely that any soldiers attacked and killed will be Sinhalese, though in the past Tamil soldiers also have been singled out and killed.

The army truck in which the 13 soldiers were travelling on the evening of July 23rd drove into explosives. In an interview with General Atygalla, now Secretary to the Ministry of Defence, we were told that the army patrol in question had changed its route at the last minute and that no-one knew why this had happened. The patrol had lost radio contact with other army personnel and had driven straight into the ambush.

All reports indicated a great deal of on-going hostility between the armed forces and the civilian population of the northern province. This is documented in more detail later in the report in Section IIA xv) and xvi).

The ambush of the 13 soldiers was carried out in this climate of tense hostility. Quite apart from the general animosity which was reported, there were allegations that the ambush was in retaliation to a very recent raping of several Tamil girls by soldiers.

iii) Events in Jaffna following the ambush

On the morning following the ambush, from very early in the morning, (4.30 a.m. or so), according to lawyers, doctors, politicians, government employees, students and citizens in Jaffna, the army went on a rampage and shot, killed and injured civilians, starting with small boys going to tutory classes early in the morning, and the violence continued throughout the day.

Soldiers travelling in an army truck were said to have struck a cyclist and run over him. The truck overturned, the soldiers then took over a private minibus, having ordered the 12 or 13 people inside to get down. The soldiers then drove to Manipaya where they stopped a civilian bus, ordered the passengers to get out, separating youths and schoolboys from the women and old people, and shooting at the males. Several died on the spot and one person died later in hospital.

These same soldiers are then reported to have stopped another minibus. This time they did not order people to get out but fired into the bus, reportedly killing 3 people instantly and wounding several others. Two of the wounded persons were reported to have died later at Chankani Hospital. One of them was said to be a journalist and newspaper editor. Another of those shot, Mr. A. Vimalathasan, was a full-time working member of MIRJE, (the Movement for Inter-Racial Justice and Equality).

Shots were fired indiscriminately as the army truck was driven along and people standing near the doors of their houses were killed and wounded. One person was killed at Chandilipai and another at Pandatherupu. Some soldiers were reported to have gone into houses and to have shot people inside at point blank range. We met the families of several victims who had been killed in this way, and were left in no doubt that in their cases this had happened. Most of those selected to be shot were men and boys.

We heard allegations by many people, including two doctors, that, following this violence 51 bodies were taken to the Jaffna hospital and that more people were killed in fact, but that in some cases the relatives and friends of those killed were too frightened to report the deaths and take the bodies to hospital. They feared further reprisals as a consequence of attracting attention to themselves. Also, families without cars needed to hire a car in order to transport a body to the hospital, and it appears that the people who hired out cars were reluctant to perform this service, so that this was a further reason for the private disposal of bodies.

We were told that 60 or more people in total were killed in and around Jaffna by the army immediately after the ambush, and that many more were wounded. Also we were told that yet more people were killed on subsequent days.

Although it was not possible to ascertain the precise number of people killed and injured by soldiers on July 24th, it is clear that many unarmed and innocent civilians were shot and killed or wounded on that day. We met people with personal knowledge of killings which took place on July 24th within their immediate neighbourhood. As many as 12 were known to have been killed within one very small neighbourhood and we met several people with direct knowledge of the deaths which took place in this area. One of the people interviewed gave us a list of the names of some of those killed who had been known personally to him.

No inquest was carried out on most of the bodies of those killed in Jaffna during these episodes. Members of the security forces said that under Regulation 15A of the emergency regulations (discussed later, under the heading: other emergency regulations, Section IIIB iv)) inquests were not necessary, so the bodies, after being taken to the morgue, were handed over to relatives for burial, or were cremated or buried by the police or armed forces without inquest. This, of course, makes the collection of reliable evidence much more difficult.

However, one inquest was being carried out by Judge Wigneswaran, a District Court judge, on the ground that Regulation 15A only applies to deaths which occur as a result of activities performed by the army in the course of duty, and that, since the soldiers were travelling in a civilian van they must first prove that their actions fell under the emergency regulations, otherwise an inquest is necessary. This inquest was into the death of one of the men shot while alighting from a bus on July 24th and who died later from his injuries in a nearby nursing home. The nursing home was in Judge Wigneswaran's jurisdiction. The Jaffna morgue is in a different jurisdiction.

The killing of the 13 soldiers was reported immediately by the media, and the names of the soldiers were published, but the killing of the civilians by the soldiers on the following day was not reported. Had the deaths of civilians in Jaffna on July 24th been reported events might have turned out very differently. Two weeks later the President in answer to a question asked at a press conference is reported to have said that he had heard that some 20 civilians in Jaffna had been killed by troops on a rampage, and indicated at that time that he had then only just been informed of the killings. Even then that information was not made public in Sri Lanka. It was, however, published in the British newspaper, *The Guardian*, and in other foreign newspapers, and several people whom we met had learned of it from those sources.

Speaking of another incident which had involved the stopping of a bus in search of militants, and the killing of persons inside, a government spokesman was reported, in the international media, to have said that the victims probably had no connection with terrorism.

On August 22nd,1983, in a statement to the UN Sub-Commission on the Prevention of Discrimination and Protection of Minorities, Ambassador Tissa Jayakody said that there had been no mass killings by the armed forces as alleged, but that "the armed forces have killed 37 persons in the Northern Province in the course of operations following the ambush of July 23rd".

iv) Incidents at the Kanatte Cemetery
The government arranged for the bodies of the 13 ambushed soldiers to be brought to Colombo for a mass burial which was to be held at the Kanatte Cemetery on the evening of the day following the ambush, that is, Sunday, 24th July. Apparently it was felt that the occasion of 13 separate funerals in the different areas from which the soldiers came

might lead to trouble at each of those funerals, whereas, if the burials all took place in the one area, a multiplicity of tensions would be avoided. One of the reasons for the anticipation of trouble was that the bodies of the soldiers had been badly disfigured in the explosion, and it was thought that their return in this state to their families would increase the level of hostility already felt at their deaths. The plan was to bury the soldiers together without handing over the bodies first to their relatives.

As a result of the decision to bury the soldiers in Colombo many people, relatives and friends and villagers from the homes of the soldiers, collected at the cemetery. Many people who would have attended the funerals had they been held in the separate birth-places of the soldiers, had come to Colombo to attend the ceremony there instead. There may have been as many as 300 persons from each area and, in addition of course, many other people from Colombo were at the cemetery as well.

According to observers the crowd which collected (reported in one paper as consisting of 10,000 people) was restive. There was a delay in the arrival of the bodies, and, by the time of their arrival, feelings were running very high.

We were told that the police were responsible for the funeral arrangements and that soldiers were hindering them and objecting to the digging of the graves for their 13 fellow soldiers, that statements were made protesting about the fact that there was no arrangement for burial with military honours, (although a government spokesman did later indicate that the funerals were intended to be with military honours), and that the feeling developed that it was an affront to bury these people who had died on duty in a mass burial at night, particularly as the bodies of the militants are generally returned to their families for burial.

Throughout the large crowd there was a general feeling of intense resentment about the fact that Sinhalese soldiers had been murdered by Tamil militants. It was said that this resentment and hostility was being deliberately fanned by certain segments of the crowd. This feeling, of course, was not tempered by any knowledge of the killings of Tamil civilians already carried out in revenge by the armed forces in Jaffna, as this information had not been made public.

As time passed feelings grew higher, the villagers and relatives began demanding that the bodies be returned to them. Meanwhile the delays, and the lack of information being relayed to the people at the cemetery, combined to make matters worse. Because the crowd became so restless, despite the government's original intention, the bodies of the soldiers were eventually returned to their relatives.

v) Commencement of the violence in Colombo

Violence began late in the evening of 24th July, at a district in Colombo called Borella, which is where the cemetery is located. The crowd became incensed and began to move into other areas near to the cemetery. Attacks began and went on until the following morning. The violence was directed against the property of Tamils. Shops owned by Tamils were set on fire and Tamil houses were burned, furniture and goods were destroyed. On the first evening, and indeed during the first day or two, the violence consisted mainly of this destruction of property.

Whereas, in the past, communal violence had been sporadic and spontaneous and directed against people, the violence now was not of this nature but clearly directed against property, means of livelihood and production. The aim of the first attacks was destruction only, though looting did follow. However, it seems that the looting was carried out by gangs different to those involved in the destruction. It was reported by many people, including some Sinhalese, that in some instances students from Buddhist schools followed on behind the first rioters and that some Buddhist monks were seen amongst the gangs.

I met several Tamil families whose houses had been burned and belongings destroyed, who had lost all their possessions except for the clothes they were wearing at the time. Some specific accounts of individual incidents told to me are reproduced elsewhere in this report. They are typical of many other first hand accounts that I heard from different individuals and families.

In addition to the destruction of the possessions, houses and flats of Tamil people, many Tamil-owned businesses and factories as well as smaller shops and boutiques were destroyed as well. Apart from the loss caused in the actual destruction, this has also produced the consequence that thousands of jobs have ceased to exist.

Very many of those rendered jobless are Sinhalese. The disaster has not had adverse consequences for the Tamils alone. Thousands of Sinhalese have, as a result of the destruction of Tamil property, suffered severe dislocation in their own lives. For instance very early in the week of violence, 40 Tamil-owned factories around Colombo were reported to have been destroyed with the loss of 25,000 jobs and, after the violence, Mr. Premadasa, the Prime Minister, was reported to have stated that 150,000 jobs had been lost, and that 90% of these jobs belonged to Sinhalese people.

It must be noted that there is no doubt that the Sinhalese population as a whole was not involved in the violence, that only sections of it were involved. I heard many accounts of Sinhalese sheltering 20 or even more Tamil friends in their houses, and many Tamils to whom I spoke said they owed their lives to Sinhalese rescuers, and that in many instances Sinhalese had risked their own lives to protect Tamil people.

Also, it was evident that this help was not confined to the week of violence but that, since the violence ceased, many Sinhalese have been tireless in their efforts to care for the Tamils in the camps, to look after them in their own neighbourhoods and to help to rehouse them. Many Sinhalese to whom I spoke were clearly shocked, distressed and sickened by what had happened.

vi) Violence in centres other than Colombo

The violence which had broken out in different parts of Colombo almost simultaneously on the night of July 24th and on July 25th, extended during the course of the next few days to different centres throughout the country. About 130 sailors broke camp in Trincomalee, a large port on the east coast, and went on a rampage in which 175 buildings were reported to have been damaged. Several people were injured and one person was reported killed.

Violence erupted also in places such as Kandy, Matale, Nuwara Eliya, Badulla and Bandarawella. On each of these occasions it followed a similar pattern. The incidents were started off by people coming in from outside the districts, lists were used to identify Tamil property and systematic attacks were made upon it: the local people were then encouraged to follow with further depradations.

The uniformity of this pattern has led to allegations that there was considerable organisation behind the events. Many people interviewed were of the opinion that, although the eruption of violence may have been triggered off by the reaction to the ambush of the 13 soldiers, this was only the flash-point and that, had that ambush not occurred, something else would have acted as a catalyst to spark off the violence.

vii) The violence and the course it took

Senior members of the government, members of opposition parties, lawyers, members of citizens' groups, people affected by the violence, and international aid workers interviewed were all consistent in stating that, from the beginning of the disturbances, many people in the mobs in the streets possessed election lists containing the names and addresses of all those who lived in particular streets. The lists indicated the houses in occupation by Tamils and also whether the owner of a house was Tamil, Sinhalese or Muslim. The possessions and houses of Tamil people were then systematically attacked. If a Tamil family were living in a house rented from Sinhalese owners the house itself was not damaged but the furniture and property of the Tamils within it would be destroyed. In many streets all the Tamil-owned shops were destroyed but those owned by Muslims or Sinhalese were spared. The same thing happened with houses.

The destruction was repeatedly described as systematic and organised. Similar lists were used in all the towns where violence occurred throughout the country. These lists were several years old. As a result sometimes the gangs using them went to houses no longer occupied by the persons named on the list.

Eye-witnesses and victims reported that on the streets cars were stopped by gangs, and the people inside were asked whether they were Sinhalese or Tamil. Some Sinhalese words are extremely difficult for people who do not speak the language fluently to pronounce; people were tested by being made to pronounce these words. The mobs were demanding to see identity cards to establish whether or not people were Tamils. Both Sinhalese and Tamils reported being stopped and questioned in this way. All found it a terrifying experience.

People identified as Tamils as a result of the questioning were told to get out of their cars, and their cars were set alight. If they were Sinhalese they were allowed to go, although often demands were made for petrol from the car, and the petrol was then used in the destruction of Tamil property. Early in the week the mobs were relatively orderly; later in the week many of the aggressors were reported to be drunk, having rifled liquor stores. This made the encounters even more terrifying for those stopped.

Threats of personal harm were being made in the first few days, and indeed being made very forcibly. For instance people recounted having sharp knives placed against their throats while they were being questioned. However, on the whole, as long as there was no resistance, the destruction was confined to property, though undoubtedly there were instances of injuries and deaths during that period. I was told that the first arrivals at the displaced persons' camps were generally physically unharmed, and that those who were injured tended to have incurred their injuries by jumping from windows, or scaling walls when fleeing, rather than as a result of direct attacks.

In cases where any resistance was offered killings were likely to take place. One instance was reported to have occurred in the town of Badulla where all the members of a Tamil family were said to have been killed. I heard of other instances also in which members of the armed forces were said to have disarmed anyone who offered resistance and then to have allowed the mobs to do with the people as they pleased.

From the morning of July 25th onwards, in broad daylight on the highways from Mount Lavinia to Bambalpitiya (two miles from the Fort area in central Colombo), eye-witnesses said that Tamil-owned businesses of whatever type — grocery shops, small kiosks, hotels etc. — were being gutted in the presence of the security forces. Attacks in all these areas took place at about the same time.

A curfew was imposed at 2 p.m. on Monday July 25th. The curfew had originally been intended for 6 p.m. but it was brought forward to 2 p.m. as the violence was so extreme. Many people felt that it should have been imposed very much earlier.

On Tuesday, the 26th July, a curfew was imposed throughout the whole day. Despite this, people were still roaming the streets, and the violence continued. An Editorial in *The Daily News* (a Sri Lankan paper) contained the following comment on the curfew:

" The older generation will recall Gray's meticulously polished lines which sang of the curfew tolling the knell of parting day and leaving the world to darkness and to me.

It is the sad truth of recent experience, however, that, in many areas, the curfew imposed by the state left the world to darkness — but not always to anyone in splendid isolation.

We have seen the effects of humbug and hypocrisy in our times; of duplicity by leaders in the North and of equal sham by public figures in the South.

We have seen men enjoying positions of responsibility conniving with hoodlums and rowdies, in some cases actively inciting violence.

Either we admit to these facts and correct them, or we will deceive ourselves again until there is another breakdown of law and order.

It is a known truth that people, who have used devious methods to discredit the law and its institutions, staged massive attacks on men and houses under cover of the curfew.

If we are to salvage ourselves, our country from the destruction and tensions that loom over the present scene, we may as well begin by facing up to the truths of the past weeks.

In the suburbs especially, in some cases under the very shadow of the City, gangs broke into houses and plundered — once the curfew came into force. For it meant that they were less likely to be seen or detected. They were, generally, sure that no patrols would appear to challenge them.

The law, to be respected, must be enforced and enforced without fear or favour. There are people, probably, who fancy that they have the wit to flirt with thugs and thuggery, take what they want out of them, as one might of people of easy virtue, and then maintain a firm hand over them.

To be so deluded is to ignore the lessons of history: to ignore the teachings of great religious leaders, to set moral values at naught.

Thus, for the future, if we are to survive as a nation worthy of our long culture and heritage, we must re-furbish the image of law and order in this land: we must re-erect the figure of justice.

To be brutally frank, what we saw two weeks ago was a brief reign of terror at the hands of lawless elements. Were they acting to any pattern? If so, who drew up that strategy?

We have rounded up a fair number of looters. Have we still to trace the arsonists, the sword wielding, incendiary throwing seerayas? Will we ever?

Plainly, there can be no security, no progress, no civilisation without public security not merely in name but in eminent practice as well. To begin with the curfew must never again be allowed to look like a piece of poetic licence, if we may take some liberty with the expression, to describe a sad deformity." (August 20th 1983).

During the last week of July the curfew was often imposed for a whole twenty-four hours, though, periodically during the day, it would be lifted for a few hours to enable people to purchase food. Banks and shops had all been closed and many people, particularly those who do not purchase more food than they use each day, were experiencing severe food shortages.

In an attempt to curb the disturbances the government continued to impose curfews, and indeed they were still being enforced, although for more restricted periods, when we were in Sri Lanka at the end of August.

viii) The role played by the security forces

Many eye-witnesses said that on the morning of Monday July 25th they saw scarcely any members of the armed forces on the streets, just a few policemen, and that the police who were present were turning a blind eye to what was happening. There were conflicting opinions as to whether this was because the security forces were co-operating with the mob, or simply that they were unable to cope with the crowds as they were so outnumbered.

Later that day soldiers in great numbers did appear and the curfew was imposed. However, eye-witnesses reported that, although the soldiers were now on the streets they did not make any attempt to check the violence, that they stood by at the very least, and actively participated at the worst, in the violence which was being perpetrated against the Tamil people.

The explanation given for this was that the militants had been killing members of the army, and that the armed forces were very resentful at what they considered to be a lack of action against the militants by the Sri Lankan government, at the restrictions on their powers when dealing with the militants, and also very resentful towards Tamil people in general. They had the feeling that revenge should be taken for the deaths suffered at the hands of the militant groups.

It should be noted that the Tamil people affected by the violence in Colombo, and in many of the other centres where violence occurred, have had nothing to do with the militant movement. They live and work with Sinhalese people, and, for the most part, are not interested in leaving their present places of residence to go to live in Eelam (the separate state advocated by some Tamils) even if it should be formed.

In the words of the Prime Minister, Mr. Premadasa,

"Can anyone be so senseless as to think that he was hitting at the terrorists in the north by harrassing harmless, innocent Tamil people in the south for the crimes of the terrorists?"

As far as I could ascertain no members of the armed forces were injured during the July week of violence, apart, of course, from the 13 soldiers killed in the ambush in Jaffna. The accounts are consistent in stating that the behaviour of the security forces improved after the first few days, most of the people to whom I spoke expressing the opinion that by then the soldiers felt that they had got their revenge for the ambush of the 13 in Jaffna. Also by the end of the week volunteer reserves were brought in and they are reported to have reacted better to discipline.

After the first few days the security forces did begin to patrol the streets, to obey orders and to enforce control. They began to prevent looting and to prevent violations of the curfew. In fact extremely strong measures were now taken. Amongst these measures was the action of shooting at offenders, and, in a government censored report of July 29th, many of those listed as killed were reported shot by police and troops for these two reasons.

ix) The Welikade prison massacres

In addition to the events recorded above there were 2 violent massacres in the Welikade prison in Colombo during which 53 Tamil prisoners, arrested on suspicion of terrorist activity, were killed. The setting in which the prison riots occurred was as follows: there were between 800 and 850 convicted prisoners in the prison, some of these prisoners were Tamils though most were Sinhalese. These 800 or so prisoners had been convicted in the ordinary courts of non-political crimes, and such people comprised the prison's usual population. At the time of the riots these prisoners were housed in the galleries and cells in the upper section of the Welikade prison. On average there were 3 prisoners in each cell.

In addition to the above prisoners, there were also in the gaol at this time 73 Tamil political prisoners who had been arrested under the *Prevention of Terrorism Act*. These people had been detained originally in army custody at Panagoda Army Camp, but recently had been transferred to the Welikade prison.

The reason for the transfer was that complaints had been made about the treatment which such detainees received whilst being held in army custody. Such complaints have been documented by Amnesty International in a report on a visit made early in 1982, by Professor Virginia Leary in a report for the International Commission of Jurists (ICJ) in 1981, and by Tim Moore MLA who prepared a report for the Australian Section of the ICJ in June 1983. The government has denied the accuracy of the complaints. Arrangements nevertheless had been made to transfer prisoners from army custody to civilian prisons, and, in June 1983, the 73 Tamil political prisoners in question had been moved to Welikade gaol.

Of these 73, some had been convicted under the *Prevention of Terrorism Act*, some were awaiting trial, and against some no charges at all had been made. Those yet to be charged or tried were being held under detention orders under the authority of the Act. In the debate in

Parliament on August 4th Mr. A. Bandaranaike stated that 30 of these prisoners were still awaiting trial (Hansard, August 4th p.1361).

The *Prevention of Terrorism Act* gives wide powers of detention without trial, and has been severely criticised for the lack of protection which it provides for those held under its provisions. (It is considered in some detail later, under the heading: *Prevention of Terrorism Act*, Section IIIB vi).

Most of the 73 prisoners were housed not with the other prisoners in the upper section, but in separate cells on the ground floor of the prison in a part called the Chapel Section. A few of them were held in a different section in a separate building, the Youthful Offenders Building. Mr. A.L. de Silva, the Superintendant of Prisons, when testifying to the magisterial enquiry of July 26th, described the accommodation arrangements as follows,

"there were 800 to 850 prisoners in the galleries and cells referred to in the upstairs portion, but the prisoners handed over to me from army custody consisting of about 73 in number were housed on the ground floor in the wings referred to which are identified as B3, C3, and D3. On July 25th I housed these prisoners as follows: 6 in B3, appellants convicted of murder. 29 detainees in D3 and 28 detainees in C3. Of the 73 referred to the balance were kept in a separate section in a separate building."

In the massacre which occurred on July 25th all of the prisoners held in B3 and D3 were massacred and killed.

The prison is located in a densely populated and poor area of the city. Mr. Mervyn Wijesinghe, Secretary to the Ministry of Justice, told us that, on July 25th, noisy, violent crowds collected in the vicinity of the prison. They were shouting and rioting and a highly charged atmosphere was created. The prisoners could hear the angry crowds outside and could see smoke and flames from the destruction of property which was going on all over the city. Tension grew and, at about 2 p.m., between 300 and 400 prisoners rioted, and forced their way into the Chapel Section. There, wielding implements said to consist of clubs and iron bars, they attacked and murdered the Tamil political prisoners. Parts of the iron supports from railings around the gallery area had been torn out and were being used as weapons. The different accounts we heard indicated that the prison guards were either unable or unwilling to control the outbreak of violence.

The report given by Mr. Jansz, the Acting Commissioner of Prisons, to the magisterial enquiry was as follows:

"As I came to the entrance to the Chapel Section prisoners were blocking the entrance, I observed about 300-400 prisoners in a state of great unrest jammed in the main lobby with clubs, iron rods and other weapons in their hands. The galleries of the upper floor were also crowded with prisoners who were inciting the prisoners in the lobby with loud shouts. With difficulty I managed to force myself into the lobby. I observed that even the wings leading to the several cells were jammed with several prisoners. I observed Mr. Silva, Superintendant of the Prison, trying to control the crowd which seemed to be overpowering him. I myself used force in trying to control the mob, some with weapons were trying to assault people on the ground. I tried to prevent it by using force, but I was helpless in the situation. I observed a few army personnel standing in the lobby and they were also helpless and could not do anything. When I realised that nothing could be done I left the building through the main entrance and got into a car which was parked in the headquarters and went to the Borella Police Station".

Mr. Jansz then recounted his attempts to obtain assistance, but none of the Inspectors at the Police Station could provide him with any personnel. He then contacted Mr. Sundaralingam, the Deputy Inspector-General, but even he could not help. Requests for help were made also to the armed forces. We were told by General Atygalla, the Secretary for the Ministry of Defence, that troops are not used inside the prison but are used only to perform guard duties at the main gate and on the perimeters. He said that when the calls for help were received it was impossible to send in a contingent immediately as there were disturbances throughout the city at the time and the forces were all deployed elsewhere.

Mr. M. Wijesinghe, Secretary to the Ministry of Justice, went to the prison and talked to the prisoners in an endeavour to restore calm. Members of the armed forces and police did arrive eventually, but by the time they were present in any number the riots had been quelled. According to the evidence given at the magisterial enquiry some of the prisoners had helped bring the situation back under control. Indeed it was stated that some of them throughout had endeavoured to restore calm but it was reported that, in the prevailing circumstances, they, and the guards, were helpless. As well Mr. Mervyn Wijesinghe told us that some of the prisoners had helped re-establish order.

Before calm was restored 35 Tamil prisoners detained under the *Prevention of Terrorism Act*, (all those housed in sections B3 and D3 of the Chapel Section of the prison), had been killed. No Sinhalese prisoners were killed, nor were any of the Tamil prisoners held in the prison as a result of conviction for ordinary crimes, attacked. We were told by Mr. Wijesinghe that there were nearly 200 Tamil prisoners in the gaol convicted of ordinary crimes, as opposed to being held under the *Prevention of Terrorism Act*, and that some of them were sharing cells with the prisoners taking part in the massacre, but that these Tamil prisoners were not harmed.

On the 26th July the Chief Magistrate of Colombo, Mr. K.S. Wijewardena, completed an investigation into the massacres but his enquiries did not reveal the identity of those responsible for the killings.

The following people were present at the enquiry, firstly, members of the Police Force: Mr. H.Y. de Silva, D.S.S.P. Crimes Colombo; Mr. T.A. Pakeer, D.A.S.P. Crimes (South); Inspector Neville Perera, O.I.C., Colombo Fraud Bureau; and Inspector Felix Silva of C.F.B. The following representatives from the Prison Authority were present: Mr. C.T. Jansz, The Deputy Commissioner of Prisons and Mr. A.L. de Silva, Superintendent of Prisons, Welikade. The following people gave evidence at the enquiry: Mr. A.L. de Silva; Mr. C.T. Jansz; two Tamil prisoners, Mr. T. Maheswaran and Mr. G. Gnanasegaran (these prisoners had been in C3 block, were unharmed and had been able to see very little of what was happening); Mr. L.D. Jayatissa, the gaol guard; and Second Leiutenant M. Hathurusinghe of the Fourth Regiment of the Sri Lanka Artillery.

The Chief Magistrate of Colombo made the following findings in relation to the death of the first 13 prisoners whose cases he examined:

"On the evidence recorded by me, it is quite clear that on the day in question, namely 25 July 1983, there had been general unrest amongst the 800 (approximately) prisoners housed on the upper floor of the Chapel Section of the Welikade Prison, which had ended up as a riot. The prisoners had stormed into the wings on to the ground floor (B3 and D3) containing the deceased prisoners. Violence had erupted, resulting in the death of the 13 prisoners referred to above. There is no evidence to identify any suspect from amongst the prisoners who had so stormed into the wings. There is evidence that some prisoners had attempted to curb the violence by assisting the authorities. None of the prison officers or the army officers summoned to the scene thereafter could have done anything under the circumstances to prevent the attack. They had all been completely overpowered. None of those prisoners who could have been eyewitnesses to the incident have volunteered to give evidence before me today. The two who have testified are not eyewitnesses and have admitted that they had seen nothing. I have perused the post mortem reports of the 13 deceased prisoners tendered before me now and I hold that the death of the 13 deceased prisoners, on the basis of evidence led are all cases of homicide. I therefore direct that the OIC of Borella Police Station conduct further investigations and report facts to the Magistrates Court of Colombo and produce suspects if any before the Chief Magistrate. On the evidence led, it is quite clear that the death of the 13 prisoners referred to are all cases of homicide as a result of a riot in prison. I shall make my finding in respect of the other deceased as and when the post mortem reports are filed before me."

The Magistrate went on to make similar findings in relation to the deaths of the other 22 prisoners who were killed in the prison on July 25th.

At the end of this enquiry Mr. H.Y. de Silva, the Detective Superintendent of Police in Colombo, acting under Regulation 15A of the emergency regulations, made an application to take into his possession the bodies of the 35 deceased prisoners for disposal in accordance with the Regulation. Mr. T. Marapona, Deputy Solicitor General, stated that he had no objection to this application. The Chief

Magistrate therefore ordered that the bodies of all 35 deceased prisoners be handed over to Mr. de Silva as requested. (Regulation 15A is discussed more fully under the heading: Other emergency regulations, Section IIIB iv).

After this first massacre the prison authorities moved from the Chapel Section the remaining 28 Tamil political prisoners who had survived. All of these persons had been in the C3 Section. They were moved now to a separate building some distance away, and were housed on the ground floor of the Youthful Offenders Building. The other Tamil political prisoners were already housed here and these prisoners were now moved upstairs. The move was reported to have been carried out in an attempt to provide greater protection to the Tamil political prisoners.

When I asked why the prisoners were not immediately removed from the gaol in view of the obvious danger they were in, I was told by a government spokesman that a second riot was simply not anticipated. He added that in any case it was not possible, because of all the troubles elsewhere, to evacuate the Tamil prisoners at this stage, as it would have been necessary to provide strict security if they were to be safely moved through the prison since the other prisoners had such violent feelings towards them.

Many of the people to whom I spoke, particularly Tamil people, lawyers and politicians, expressed grave reservations about the failure of the authorities to move the Tamil prisoners out of the prison, or at least to provide adequate security to ensure their safety, after the tragic events of July 25th.

In Parliament on August 4, Mr. A. Bandaranaike (member of the SLFP), said:

"The Government should have immediately removed every single Tamil prisoner who was held there to another place. But they did not do that. 48 hours later, another 17 Tamil prisoners were slaughtered. I am not holding a brief for those terrorists and I do not condone their acts but when they are detainees they come under the custody of the Government. It was the bounden duty of the Government to safeguard the lives of its prisoners." (Hansard, August 4, p. 1361).

As it was, the prisoners remained in the Welikade prison and, in the afternoon of July 27th, there was a second massacre in which 17 more of the remaining 37 Tamil political prisoners were killed. The Prime Minister, Mr. Premadasa, in a speech in Parliament made on August 4th said that one Sinhalese prisoner also had been killed (Hansard, August 4, p.1285). Two further Tamil prisoners were severely wounded. One of these wounded men later died in hospital, making the total killed on this second occasion 18 in number. The other wounded man, Saravan Perumal Yogarajah, was able to give evidence at the second magisterial enquiry but said that he had not recognised any of his assailants as individuals known to him, other than that they were other prisoners.

On the occasion of the second massacre the implements used by the rioting prisoners appear to have been seized from the carpentry work shop: they were described as clubs, poles and axes. By this stage additional armed forces had been stationed outside the prison and we were told by General Atygalla that this time a commando force was sent in immediately, that tear gas was used, the prisoners were brought under control, and that the commandos had rescued the remaining political prisoners who were in danger.

At the inquest carried out into the second riot Mr. Jansz, the Deputy Commissioner of Prisons gave evidence that he, from his own enquiries and from information received from his chief gaoler, did suspect that further attacks would be made on the Tamil political prisoners, and that all along he had intended the transfer of these persons to the Youthful Offenders Section to be a temporary measure lasting only until arrangements could be made for their evacuation. He told the enquiry that these arrangements had heen finalised by 2 p.m. on July 27th and that the plan was then to move the prisoners to a gaol in the town of Batticoloa, which is in the eastern province, that the availability of two air-force planes had been arranged for this purpose and that, having finalised these arrangements, Mr. Jansz returned to the prison headquarters about 4.30 p.m. that afternoon to find that a second wave of riots had broken out.

In evidence given to the second magisterial enquiry, the chief gaoler, Mr. W.M. Karunaratane, testified that he had anticipated further attacks on the Tamil prisoners and also an attempt at a mass gaol break. He had communicated these fears to his superiors. His evidence was as follows:

"I remember the 27th July 1983. On that day through the intelligence system I maintain, I gathered that tension was generally building up amongst the prison population. According to the information I gathered I anticipated two things. Firstly, that there would be an attempt to cause harm to the minority community within the prison and, secondly that an attempt would be made for a mass scale organized gaol break. I am aware that in the Welikade prison on that day we were having in our custody several terrorist prisoners. In fact on that day we had in our custody 37 terrorist prisoners. They were either suspects pending charges including murder and those detained by the Ministry in respect of terrorist activities on detention orders. All these 37 prisoners were of the minority Tamil community and in view of the prevailing communal disturbances I anticipated that they would be an obvious target of an attack. I had therefore made representations to the Acting Commissioner of Prisons, Mr. Jansz, on this basis and I am aware of the steps which were being contemplated whereby these 37 terrorist prisoners were to be evacuated. I am also aware that acting on my representations and the prevailing situation in the country, the government was taking steps to have these prisoners evacuated as early as possible. Further on the basis of the information I received I made representations to the army personnel who were engaged in security duty on the outer perimeter of the Welikade Prison to strengthen that security. I also took steps to strengthen the prison security. My representations through the army personnel were made to prevent the proposed mass scale gaol break that I anticipated on the basis of the information received. In this second massacre 17 Tamil political prisoners were killed."

According to the transcript the following people gave evidence at the second magisterial enquiry, which was again conducted by Mr. K.S. Wijewardena the Chief Magistrate for Colombo: Mr. W.A. Don Alfred, Prison Overseer; Mr. M.E. Tilakeratne, Vocational Instructor from a bakery section of the prison; Mr. P.A.B. Don Nicholas, Gaol Guard; Mr. S. Karunaratne, Gaol Guard; Mr. N.W. Katugampola, Gaol Guard; Mr. W.M. Karunaratne, Chief Gaoler; Mr. S.P. Yogarajah, the Tamil political prisoner who was injured but survived the attack; Mr. S.D. Pieris, a major in the army; Mr. C.T. Jansz, Deputy Commissioner of Prisons and Mr. W.A.L. Silva, Gaoler.

From the list of those participating in the enquiries it can be seen that lawyers for the surviving Tamil prisoners and the other surviving Tamil prisoners, (Mr Yogarajah apart), were not present at the hearing. From the evidence it would seem that on this second occasion the Tamil survivors very probably could have identified some of their assailants. On the first occasion such identification seems to have been less likely as the surviving prisoners had all been locked into one block into which very few of the attackers had entered. However, on the second occasion the prisoners were all in the same building and many of them may have had the opportunity to see who their assailants were, or to have been able to provide other evidence of assistance to the inquiry.

One of these 18 murdered prisoners was Dr. Rajasunderam, a medical practitioner and Secretary of the Gandhiyam movement. Dr. Rajasunderam's case had been featured in the Amnesty International July 1983 Newsletter. The Gandhiyam movement is a social services organisation. Its members had been helping to resettle Tamil displaced persons who had fled to the northern part of the country as a result of earlier disturbances which have taken place in Sri Lanka in recent years. Accusations have been made by the government to the effect that this organisation has links with the militants. Dr. Rajasunderam and his wife had devoted a great amount of work and time to helping these displaced persons and also in working to assist disadvantaged members of the Indian Tamil community. Dr. Rajasunderam had been arrested under the the *Prevention of Terrorism Act* in April 1983, accused of "association with Tamil terrorists". Since then he had been held without charge or trial. It was reported by Amnesty International that in May he had been beaten up in the Panagoda Army Camp where he was being held incommunicado. The report of the Judicial Medical Officer showed that he had sustained injuries as a result of his treatment there.

Accounts of the Welikade massacres were given later to journalists by some of the Tamil prisoners who survived the second attack, after they escaped from Batticoloa gaol (to which they were now transferred). One of the accounts was given by Mr. S.A. David, the President of The Ghandiyam movement. He had been arrested with Dr. Rajasunderam in April 1983. His description of the Welikade prison massacres, as recorded by a journalist, was as follows:

Prison Slaughter
On July 25, 1983 the Sinhala prisoners attacked the detainees in the Chapel Section of the prison and murdered 35 persons among whom were Kuttimany, Jegan and Thangathurai. From eye witness accounts, Kuttimany's eyes were gouged and his blood drunk by his attackers. After killing six Tamils including Kuttimany in one wing, the attackers killed 29 Tamils in the other wing. A boy of 16 years, Mylvaganam, had been spared by the attackers, and was crouching in a cell. A jail guard spotted him and stabbed him to death.

The 35 dead were heaped in front of the statue of Gautama Buddha in the yard of Welikade prison, as Minister Athulathmudali so aptly described as a 'sacrifice to appease the blood thirsty cravings of the Sinhala demons'.

Some who were yet alive raised their heads and called for help but were beaten down to death in the heap.

The attackers then made entry into the other wing through openings in the first floor but the jailers there refused to give the keys and persuaded them to leave.

Second Massacre
28 Tamil detainees in this wing were transferred to the ground floor of the Youth Ward and nine of us were accommodated on the First Floor. All was quiet on the 26th. On the 27th at 2.30pm there was shouting around Youth Ward and armed prisoners scaled boundary walls and started to break open gates in the Youth Ward. Nearly 40 prisoners armed with axes, swords, crowbars, iron pipes and wooden legs appeared before our door and started to break the lock. Dr Rajasundaram walked up to the door and pleaded with them to spare us as we were not involved in any robberies or murders and as Hindus we did not believe in violence and as Buddhists they should not kill. The door suddenly opened and Dr Rajasundaram was dragged out and hit with an iron rod on the head. He fell among the crowd. The rest of us broke the chairs and tables and managed to keep the crowd at bay for half an hour. The Army arrived, threw tear gas bombs and dispersed the crowd. Then the 2 soldiers lined up 8 of us and were taking aim to shoot when the Commander called out from below to them to come down. Then the soldiers chased us down and all who escaped death were lined up on the footpath in front of the Youth Ward. As we walked out, we saw corpses of our colleagues around us and we heard prisoners shouting that it was a pity we were allowed to live.

We were ordered to run into a mini-van and removed out of the prison compound and loaded into an Army truck. We were ordered to lie face down on the floor of the truck and a few who raised their heads were trampled down

by the soldiers. All along the way to Katunayake Airport some soldiers kept cursing the Tamils and Eelam and using obscene language. We were kept at the airport until early morning. We were refused even water. We were then taken into an Air Force plane, ordered to sit with our heads down until we reached Batticoloa Airport. From there we were taken in an open van to Batticoloa prison. Here, we were received with sympathy and smiles. Hot tea was served to us. We felt we had returned to sanity and some measure of safety."
(*The Tamil Times*, November 1983.)

Another account, that of Mr. K. Devanandan, contained the following description:

"Giving the first eye-witness account of the Welikade massacres of July 25th and 27th, Mr. Devanandan said that but for the intervention of a Muslim army commander, none of the Tamil political prisoners would have survived. The July 25 massacre was conducted at 2.30 p.m. when Colombo was under total curfew. Air force helicopters hovered over the jail when the killings took place inside, under the supervision of the deputy jail superintendent, aided and abetted by the army and security guards. The July 27th killings were led by Sepala Ekanaike, undergoing life imprisonment for hijacking an Alitalia plane on its flight from Delhi to Bangkok in July last year. Sinhalese prisoners convicted on murder, rape and burglary charges were handpicked by the warders for the attack, after plying them with liquor, Mr. Devanandan said. They came out from their cells shouting "Kottiya Maranda Ona" (kill the tigers)."
(*The Tamil Times*, September-October 1983).

I heard expressions of dissatisfaction with the fact that allegations such as these indicating complicity by some prison staff were not dealt with, and many of those to whom I spoke expressed a fervent hope that the police enquiries, which Mr. K.S. Wijewardena at the conclusion of both enquiries directed to be instigated, would be held and would be both comprehensive and speedy. There was a general feeling among many of the people to whom I spoke that the government should immediately order a thorough enquiry into the two massacres.

Returning to the second enquiry, at its conclusion Mr. H.Y. de Silva, Detective Superintendant of Police Crime, Colombo, again made an application under Regulation 15A for possession of the bodies of the 18 deceased prisoners, and the Magistrate ordered that the bodies be handed over to him in accordance with that Regulation.

After this second massacre all the surviving Tamil political prisoners in Welikade prison were moved that evening under armed guard to the airport. They were flown to Batticoloa in the eastern province on the following morning, and housed in a gaol there. We were told by a member of the public service that, in addition,Tamil political prisoners from another Colombo gaol were also sent to Batticoloa in the interest of their safety. In order to provide the required accommodation an equivalent number of Sinhalese prisoners were brought from Batticoloa to Colombo.

The prisoners had to remain in Colombo at the airport overnight since planes can land at Batticoloa only in daylight hours, and it was reported that there were fears for their safety during the night since the armed forces guarding them were known to be hostile to them. However, the night passed quietly and no untoward incidents occurred.

Unfortunately we were unable to visit Batticoloa to interview the Tamil political prisoners who had survived the massacres in Welikade gaol as it was not possible in the short time that the delegation was in Sri Lanka to make the arrangements to travel there.

x) The events of July 29th

The disturbances in Colombo gradually lessened on July 27th and 28th. However, on Friday July 29th there was another very bad outbreak of violence, and this time the violence was directed not only against property but also against people. Eye-witnesses were said to have reported that a Tamil group near the Central Railway Station fired on security forces killing at least 2 soldiers. There were also reports that a hand bomb had been thrown at a security patrol and that the patrol fired back and killed 2 or more of a mob that had gathered. We were told that gun fire was heard for two hours, and that the police were reported to have taken at least 12 Tamils into custody. Rioting occurred within a few blocks of the Presidential Palace.

Rumours began to spread that a militant group known as the Tigers had come to Colombo and were in the Fort and Pettah areas, (this is the business and commercial district of Colombo). The rumours spread rapidly throughout the city. Within ten to fifteen minutes they had been heard in areas ten miles away. People were said to have driven around in vans and travelled on bicycles, spreading the news. There was great panic, people were running and driving away from the city centre and the consequence was traffic jams and chaos. Violence erupted again.

The violence on Friday July 29th was of horrifying proportions and I heard eye-witness accounts of terrible atrocities. Cars were stopped and this time if Tamils were in the cars they were burned inside them, petrol was poured over people and they were set alight, people were also burned in their houses, and were hacked to death.

This time the violence, though more extreme, was more short-lived. Order was restored and the violence ceased.

xi) Direct results of the violence

The last week of July left many dead, many injured, thousands displaced, great losses of property, economic and physical dislocation, and a shocked population.

Estimates of the number of persons killed in the week of violence vary. Official estimates are just under 400 killed. These estimates are conservative. Unofficial estimates are as high as 1,500-2,000. It is probable that many bodies were not at first discovered because they were burned in houses. Also some bodies were hidden and buried privately by people who were frightened by the prospect of further reprisals should the bodies be discovered, or scared to attract attention to themselves by reporting the deaths. At the date of our departure from Sri Lanka, September 1st, 1983, there were many people still missing or not accounted for.

A direct result of the upheavals was that a great number of people fled to the displaced persons' camps which had been set up hastily in Colombo and elsewhere.

xii) Some specific incidents suffered by individuals and families during the week of violence

The following incidents were recounted by either the individuals affected or by their close relatives. Other witnesses corroborated the information recorded below. Names have been withheld where the persons in question preferred this.

Incident A

At about 1 a.m. in the early morning of July 24th, members of a Sri Lankan Tamil family consisting of husband and wife and two small children, were awoken by banging and a lot of noise outside the door of the flat where they stayed at weekends. The flat was in an area of Colombo not far from the cemetery where the violence had begun. The husband went to the door to find a large angry mob outside armed with axes, knives, bottles, iron bars, indeed an assortment of weapons, though one thing upon which he did comment was the number of new shining knives which the people were brandishing. Immediately upon his opening the door the crowd demanded to know whether he was a Tamil or a Sinhalese. He did not reply directly to this question but replied in Sinhalese (in which language he was fluent) telling the crowd the name of the location where he currently worked and had worked for the past twenty years. This was a Sinhalese town and the place where the family home was situated.

The leaders of the mob, upon hearing him speak, assumed that he was Sinhalese and ceased their menacing behaviour. The crowd then began gradually to leave and move down the stairs. However, as this was happening, a woman, whom the family did not know, stepped forward with a piece of paper in her hands and shouted, "They are Tamils". Immediately the crowd turned, became very threatening, and pushed into the flat. Some people began to destroy things within the flat, and the fridge, stove and kitchen equipment were thrown out of the window. Other members of the mob brandished weapons as this was being done.

The family's two small children were petrified and fled to hide under one of the beds. No attempt to resist was made. Parents and children were very frightened, and the parents felt that any sign of resistance or any false move on their part could cause a loss of temper or loss of control and result in bloodshed. Finally the husband asked permission to take his wife and children out of the flat, and they were allowed to leave.

A Sinhalese family living in a flat in the same building gave them shelter for the night. Everything in the flat of the Tamil family was either destroyed that evening or looted later. When the mob left the building they asked about the ownership of the cars parked there. The Sinhalese family claimed ownership of the Tamil family's car and, as a consequence, the car was left undamaged.

Meanwhile emergency calls had been made by friends of the Tamil family who had heard that they were in trouble. They called both police headquarters and the army. Contact was made with the Inspector-General of Police and a request made that an emergency car be sent to help the family. The Inspector-General informed the callers that this was impossible as the violence was widespread and all the forces were out, so that it was out of the question to attend to specific incidents. No one was able to get an answer from the army quarters. The police had been notified of the incident at 1 a.m. At 5.30 a.m. a patrol car did come by the block of flats but did not stop.

In the early morning hours the Tamil family, fearing that their presence would endanger their Sinhalese rescuers, set off in their car to try to reach the house of a relative and ultimately to go to their own house. They had a nightmarish journey through the streets of Colombo, being frequently stopped by mobs armed with iron bars, knives, bottles, cricket stumps and other weapons, and being asked whether they were Sinhalese or Tamil. The mobs were very threatening but the family managed to get through because of their fluency in Sinhalese. At one stage the petrol was taken from their car.

After detours, several days of hiding, and great help from Sinhalese friends the family finally reached their destination only to discover that their house had been attacked and destroyed and that, after the initial destruction, it had been looted and then set alight so that only the walls remained standing.

Until this point the family had been confident that, had they been at home in the town where they had lived and worked for the past twenty years, where they had many friends and where they held respected positions in the community, they would have been safe. They were told, however, that the mob which had carried out this destruction was drunk and violent and would have killed them had they been in the house.

Their two children have been extremely badly frightened by these experiences. The seven year old son did not stop shaking for hours after the family's escape from the flat, and he began shaking again on the following day. This shaking continued for several hours. When he was asked what sort of a house he would like to live in the most important aspect to him was that all houses should have strong iron bars and heavy locks on all doors and windows.

Because the parents feel that they can never again be confident about their security in Sri Lanka, and because they do not feel they can risk their children having to face another experience like this, they, like many others to whom I spoke, expressed a strong desire to leave the country.

Incident B

I was told by a senior government official that, on Monday July 24th, at 10.30 a.m. Tamil lawyers came to the Justice Department asking for police protection. Their offices were being attacked and burnt. The Inspector-General of Police was contacted and was asked to provide police protection for the lawyers. The reply was that no help could be given as the situation was the same all over Colombo and all the forces were out.

The government official, who was Sinhalese, made ten trips in his own car to take Tamil lawyers to safety and, in the process, he also was almost massacred. He returned to his office at 6.30 p.m. shocked. He said that the city which had seemed quiet when everyone had arrived at work that morning had been in flames and total chaos by mid-day.

Incident C

The following events on July 25th befell another Tamil family living in Colombo. The head of the household, (again all members of the family spoke fluent Sinhalese and had lived in Sinhalese-dominated areas all their lives), had gone out to buy some provisions and was returning home by bus. The bus made a detour because there were large gatherings in the streets and, as a result, the gentleman alighted in a district called Narahenpita in Colombo 5. There he saw Tamil boutiques ablaze, people screaming and running, and others brandishing weapons.

He rushed back to his own house in Polhengoda Road, and when he arrived he saw a gang of several hundred people shouting and approaching his house. Only his wife and his grandaughter, a baby four months old, were inside. His daughter had left that morning for her job in the city. He rushed inside and snatched his grandchild from her cot grabbing two nappies at the same time. The clothes they wore and these two nappies are the only possessions this couple now has. The husband and his wife ran into the garden with the child. The crowd entered the house and destroyed everything in it.

The couple and child remained in the garden too terrified to move, and a couple of hours later looters arrived and began to go through the wreckage. At this point a car from the office where the daughter worked, arrived and the couple and baby were rescued. The family stayed for a few days in the office building where the daughter worked. They then went to a displaced persons' camp for almost two weeks where they experienced many problems. They particularly mentioned the inadequacy of the toilet facilities.

After this period they accepted the government's offer of transportation by ship to Jaffna. The vessel on which they travelled, a cargo boat, for some reason took five days to complete what is usually a much shorter journey. The conditions were described as being dreadful. Sometimes the people on board received biscuits to eat but mostly nothing. There was no organised provision of food and there were no toilets.

These people are now staying with relatives in Jaffna. The daughter has no job there and the family has lost its entire life savings. Since they have been in Jaffna they have heard that their house has been burned and totally destroyed.

Incident D
The following events are reported to have happened to 5 families living close to each other in Karallapona, near Colombo. Their houses were attacked and burned on July 26th. All 5 families then moved into a camp for displaced persons. In the camp the sanitary conditions were so bad that the men decided to go back to their houses to see if they could wash there. While they were doing this a crowd collected at their houses and all 5 men were hacked to death and burnt. All of them had been senior government executives. At the time no one knew why the men failed to return to the camps. Their wives and families left the camps to travel by ship to Jaffna still not knowing the fate of their husbands, but this is the report which now has been transmitted to them.

Incident E
At Badulla, a senior lawyer, Mr K. B. Nadaraja, a man now in his 80s, was in his house with his son who is also a lawyer, now employed in Germany. The son was in Badulla on holiday with his children. This family was highly respected in the district. A gang arrived and chased the family from the house. Another lawyer sheltered them, and for this act he was threatened with the same fate. The family was rescued by members of the German Embassy. Mr. Nadaraja and the rest of the family are reported now to have left Sri Lanka.

Incident F
Also at Badulla the District Judge, Judge Suntheralingam had to flee for his life and was rescued by police.

I heard many other similar accounts of disaster and, in Jaffna, heard also accounts from the families of victims who had been shot at point blank range by soldiers in their own homes on Sunday 24th July. I have not recounted any details of these particular incidents due to the fact that it might put the victims' families in some danger.

There was no suggestion that these people had any involvement with the separatist movement or with the militants.

xii) Censorship Regulations

During the whole of this period there was government censorship of all news reports. This covered both reports being transmitted by the Sri Lankan media and those being sent out of the country by representatives of the international media. Prior to the July violence censorship had already been imposed on news: for instance news concerning universities and higher education generally was being controlled following student unrest at two universities.

Mr. Douglas Liyanage, Secretary of the Ministry of State, had been, under Regulation 14 of the emergency regulations, appointed the "competent authority" for the control of information i.e. the government censor. Regulation 14 confers very wide powers. Paragraph (1) reads as follows,

"14. (1) A competent authority may take such measures and give such directions as he may consider necessary for preventing or restricting the publication in Sri Lanka or any specified area in Sri Lanka or the transmission from Sri Lanka to places outside Sri Lanka, of matter which would or might be prejudicial to the interests of national security or the preservation of public order or the maintenance of supplies and services essential to the life of the community or of matter inciting or encouraging persons to mutiny, riot or civil commotion, and directions under this paragraph may contain such incidental and supplementary provisions as appear to the competent authority to be necessary or expedient, including provision for securing that documents, pictorial representations, photographs or cinematograph films, shall, before publication, be submitted or exhibited to the competent authority."

Regulation 14 gave Mr. Liyanage inter alia the power to control all news and, as well as this, to shut down local newspapers completely and to seal their printing presses.

Mr. Liyanage told us that there are 12 national daily newspapers in Sri Lanka. In addition there are regional newspapers. Directions were issued to all newspapers and all journalists that any material concerning the disturbances must be presented for censorship before publication.

It was reported by the international media on 24th July that the government had imposed a censorship blackout on news concerning the activities and communal violence in the north, and, as the week progressed, that restrictions were becoming tighter and that descriptions of damage in Colombo were being deleted from reports. An official announcement stated that all news prejudicial to national security, the preservation of public order, maintenance of essential supplies and services or concerning incitement to civil unrest would be censored.

Later still reports of the situation and circumstances of displaced persons were restricted, and comments from opposition politicians were forbidden publication.

Several overseas reporters complained that severe limitations were being imposed upon their movements, some were allowed to move only between their hotel rooms and the censor's office. There were also complaints about the many deletions being made to news reports. The government, on the other hand, was of the opinion that the reporting of many journalists was unfair. An American journalist was expelled for breaking the censorship laws.

Many people expressed concern at the coverage by the international media. Those complaining of this did so on the grounds that it was very critical of the government; that the majority of the international papers had sympathised with the Tamils because they were the victims of the violence; that a fair and objective assessment of the situation had not been portrayed, and that the Sinhalese people as a result now had an undeservedly poor image abroad.

There was particular objection to a photograph which appeared in the British newspaper, *The Guardian*. This photograph was taken during the 1971 disturbances, but was represented by *The Guardian* to be a photograph taken during the 1983 disturbances. *The Guardian* did later publish an apology but it was felt that this apology was half-hearted and hence did not undo the damage caused by the misleading picture. (See *Ceylon Observer Editorial*, August 21st 1983).

Guidelines were laid down so that the duties of censorship could be delegated. The guidelines issued on August 2nd are as follows:

"1. No reference will be permitted to the current security situation including assessments of damage or casualties except through the daily press briefing.

2. No reference will be permitted to matters relating to internal security.

3. No reference will be permitted to the situation at Care and Welfare Centres, including the number of such Centres and the number of occupants of such Centres. (However, appeals for assistance from Government or Voluntary Organisations will be permitted.)

4. No reference will be permitted to movement of displaced persons or modes of transportation.

5. No statements will be permitted on any subject by political parties or political personalities other than statements arranged for broadcast through State media.

6. No comment will be permitted by any person on the present security or political situation.

7. No direct reference will be permitted to any foreign country — even by implication — as being responsible for the current situation."

The information sent by Mr. Liyanage to all Secretaries of Ministries on August 4th was as follows:

"CONTROL OF PUBLICATIONS

Directions issued by me to the press and other media under Regulation 14(1) of the current Emergency Regulations bring under censorship all matters relating to the following:

(1) to the tertiary education sector which includes all Universities, Polytechnics and all Institutions providing post-secondary education;

(2) to terrorism, terrorist activity or similar acts of violence in Sri Lanka or to security operations of the armed services and the police in relation to such activities; and

(3) I shall be glad if all statements issued by you and your officers, including heads of Corporations and of Statutory Bodies, are designed to conform to these guidelines.

02 All material relating to the above has to be submitted to me for censorship before publication, and guidelines have been issued to the censors functioning under the above Regulation.

03 I shall be glad if all statements issued by you and your officers, including heads of Corporations and of Statutory Bodies, are designed to conform to these guidelines.

04 I shall be grateful if the contents of this letter are also brought to the notice of your Minister."

Asked about the closure of newspapers, Mr. Liyanage said that some papers had been closed down. These included the 2 most prominent newspapers in Jaffna, one an English language paper and one a Tamil language paper, both of which had had their presses sealed under the power given by the emergency regulations.

Also, when the 3 leftist parties were proscribed on 30th July, their papers were closed and their presses had been sealed. So were those of the paper of the SLFP, (the Sri Lanka Freedom Party) though that party itself was not proscribed. Mr. A. Bandaranaike (SLFP party member) when commenting on this during the debate in Parliament on August 4th said, (Hansard p. 1360),

"It is a funny thing because since these troubles broke out on ... the 24th July, this paper has not even been printed once. — (Interruption) — Who has seen it? Furthermore there is a very strict censorship on. If you do not want anything to be published, why not censor it? Why seal the newspaper? This is something which I do not understand. If you feel that they are publishing irresponsible things, then close it down. But you closed down a newspaper that has not printed a word since this trouble broke out."

I asked Mr. Liyanage if the proprietors of the newspapers could resist a closure order and was told that it is possible for the proprietor to bring proceedings in the Supreme Court, and that many cases had in fact been brought against him. The proceedings are generally in terms that the closure of the paper was arbitrary, in excess of powers, without sufficient cause etc. If such proceedings are successful, damages are payable. The Attorney-General defends Mr. Liyanage and so far no case brought against him has been successful. Further, under Regulation 14(8), objections against certain orders made under the Regulation may be brought before an Advisory Committee consisting of persons appointed by the President.

Mr. Liyanage said that the ban on news was not total and the censorship not absolute, and gave the example that telephones were without censorship.

xiv) Government response

Another important aspect of the events of the week beginning on 23rd July is, of course, the response of the government. Mentioned later are statements made by government ministers indicating a determination that those responsible for the July disturbances should be revealed and punished. Later also will be described the accusations levied at the 3 leftist parties, their proscription, the arrest of some of their members, and the indication of involvement of a "foreign hand". (See the sub-section: Theories as to reasons for the violence, Section IIA xvii) There are other important aspects of the response made by the government and these will be briefly covered here.

Firstly, a matter which caused comment and concern was the fact that there was no statement made by any member of the government to the public for several days. As Mr. Thondaman (Minister of Rural Industrial Development and a Tamil Member of Parliament) put it, when speaking in Parliament on August 4th, (Hansard p 1354),

"For four days after the incident broke out — I do not want to blame anybody — nobody came on television or over the radio. The country was virtually burning: unprecedented acts of violence had taken place in Colombo and in the suburbs".

The President made his first broadcast on Friday, 29th July. Statements of other government ministers then followed.

The first statement made by the President on Friday, 29th July, was as follows:

"My Dear Friends,
It is with deep regret and sorrow that I address you today. When I see the destruction around me, the spate of violence that has arisen, it is very, very

distressing. This violence has been aimed particularly against the Tamil people, and it has been caused by the deep ill-feeling and the suspicion that has grown between the Sinhala and the Tamil people for several years. When there is distrust, when there are grievances, it is easy to lead people to violence, and we feel that there is an attempt to lead this violence for the purpose of destroying the political and economic progress that this Government has been able to ensure for our people.

It was from 1956 that this suspicion between the Sinhala and the Tamil people first began. In 1976 for the first time a movement for the separation of our beloved motherland, the separation of a united Lanka into two nations, was also accepted. The Sinhalese will never agree to the division of a country which has been a united nation for 2,500 years.

At first, this movement for separation was non-violent. But since 1976 it became violent. Violence increased and innocent people were murdered. Members of the Armed Services and the Police, politicians who did not agree with the movement for violence, whether they were Sinhalese or Tamil, were assassinated. It has grown to such large proportions that not a few but hundreds had been killed during this movement. Because of this violence by the terrorists, the Sinhalese people themselves have reacted. I feel that the movement for separation should have been banned long, long ago. I have also been a member of the Governments which are responsible for not banning it. I thought that in the All-Party Conference which I summoned a few days ago, which we are unable to hold, firstly, because all the parties did not accept my invitation, and secondly because of the violence and the curfew around us, I thought that at that conference I would say that we intend to implement the 1977 manifesto of the United National Party, which sought to solve some of the political problems that arose, and once we did that, we would also ask the consensus of opinion to make the division of the country illegal.

Unfortunately, we could not hold that conference. But the Government has now decided that the time has come to accede to the clamour and the national request of the Sinhala people that we do not allow the movement for division to grow any more.

The Cabinet, therefore, this morning decided that we should bring legislation, firstly, to prevent people from entering the Legislature if they belonged to a Party that seeks to divide the nation. Secondly, the legislation will make Parties that seek to divide the nation illegal or proscribe them. And once they are proscribed, the Members cannot sit in the Legislature. We will also see that those who belong to this Party or those who advocate the separation of the country lose their civic rights and cannot hold office, cannot practice professions, cannot join movements or organisations in this country.

We are very sorry that this step should be taken. But I cannot see, and my Government cannot see, any other way by which we can appease the natural desire and request of the Sinhala people to prevent the country being divided, and to see that those who speak for division are not able to do so legally."

As is apparent from the President's statement, the government had decided to amend the *Constitution* to make any profession of support for a separate state in Sri Lanka illegal. This amendment, the Sixth Amendment, was passed by Parliament in a session called to meet on

August 4th. The government, which holds 140 of the 168 Parliamentary seats, has many more than the necessary two-thirds majority of the votes of Parliament to pass an amendment to the *Constitution* and it was never in question that the Sixth Amendment would be passed. Since one of the platforms of the then major opposition party, the TULF (the Tamil United Liberation Front) consisted of support for a separate Tamil identity, the passing of this Amendment has had the consequence that the TULF MPs have relinquished their places in Parliament. All 17 members felt they could not take the required oath as to do this would be a denial of the platform on which they had been elected. (The Sixth Amendment is discussed in more detail under the heading: The Sixth Amendment, Section IIIB viii).

xv) Theories explaining the behaviour of the security forces

An observation made by many people, both Tamil and Sinhalese, about the security forces was that many of the soldiers are very young, that the army is small (the estimate General Atygalla gave was 9,000 men in the regular force, with another 2,500 in the Navy and Airforce) and that the forces are somewhat inexperienced, never having fought in a war. As a result it was said that their members treat any deaths as a source of resentment and cause for revenge. I was told that their only experience of combat was their action in bringing under control the violence and insurgency which had errupted in 1971.

In an interview with General Atygalla, Secretary of the Ministry of Defence, and Mr. Weerapittia, a former Deputy Inspector General of Police and now the Deputy Minister of Defence, I asked what the instructions to the security forces had been during the week of violence and was told that the instructions to both the armed forces and the police had been very clear — that they were to maintain law and order and to use maximum force where this was necessary.

Since these instructions appear not to have been obeyed, particularly early in the week, I asked if disciplinary measures were being taken against those members of the security forces who had failed to carry out their orders. I was told that they were not, but that, however, inquiries were being held to find out the reasons and that inquiries into incidents of injury or theft are always held.

General Atygalla said that disciplinary proceedings had been taken after the violence which had occurred in Jaffna, in May 1983, in which members of the armed forces had gone on a rampage, and that, following the proceedings, 74 soldiers had been dismissed. Also over 100 members of the navy who shortly afterwards had caused destruction in Trincomalee were said to have been disciplined. From questions asked in subsequent interviews it became clear that the general public is not always aware that disciplinary measures such as these have been taken.

Both General Atygalla and Mr.Weerapittia stressed that the background had to be borne in mind: that 13 soldiers had just been ambushed and killed, and that there had been very many brutal murders both of the members of the armed forces and of democratic politicians in the north by Tamil militants, that the soldiers received no co-operation from the people in the north when they were endeavouring to find the leaders, that they were unable to get evidence or any assistance, and that they were being killed in cold blood. It was further stated that this was not the time to proceed with inquiries because the government has to use the same troops, but that the troops have been told that if they had failed to take action this was not right and that they should not repeat this behaviour.

The public servants whom I asked whether the security forces would be disciplined for their complicity in the violence said that there had been complicity, but the government was unable to take steps to discipline the army or the police at the moment as the security forces were needed to maintain law and order, and that in any case it was very difficult to allocate responsibility for what had happened.

An Editorial in *The Times of India*, of August 10th, carried the following report:

"....Asked by a BBC correspondent why government troops drawn from the Sinhalese population had not fired on rioters attacking Tamils and destroying their homes and business [President Jayewardene] has said: 'I think there was a big anti-Tamil feeling among the forces. They also felt that shooting the Sinhalese, who were rioting, would have been anti-Sinhalese, and actually in some places we saw them encouraging (rioters)".

Many people, lawyers, members of citizens' and religious groups, aid organisations, foreign diplomats, university staff, said they felt that the government had lost control of the security forces during the first few days. In consequence there is a great feeling of insecurity amongst the Tamil population in particular, and a feeling that the government will not be able in the future to guarantee their safety any more than it was able to do so in July 1983.

One of the matters which would seem to be contributing to the problem here is the fact that so few Tamils are employed in either the police force or the armed forces. We were unable to obtain official figures, and the estimates given varied, but were between 80% and 95% Sinhalese in the police force, and up to 99% Sinhalese personnel in the army, 95-99% in the Navy, and approximately 80% Sinhalese in the Air Force.

In view of the high percentage of Sinhalese in the security forces I asked General Atygalla and Mr.Weerapittia if the hiring policy was a discriminatory one. They said not, that all advertisements for jobs were public advertisements, and that the positions were open to Tamils, but that very few Tamils applied.

It was further stressed that a disproportionate number of top positions in the police force were held by Tamils. We were told by General Atygalla and Mr.Weerapittia that, of 10 top positions, 5 were held by Tamils. We were also told that 70% of the police force in Jaffna was composed of Tamil policemen. Other estimates given to us were that 40%-50% of the police force in Jaffna were composed of Tamil policemen but that there were exceedingly few Tamil policemen elsewhere. The relations between the police and the civilian population in Jaffna were reported to have improved greatly since the number of Tamil personnel there had been increased. The army in the northern province still has a very hostile relationship with the rest of the community.

In contrast to this viewpoint, all of the Tamils to whom I spoke about recruitment for the armed forces were of the opinion that the hiring policy was discriminatory, and that it was very difficult for Tamils to get through the selection processes. Further, they pointed out that the Tamils now in top positions were hired many years ago, before the commencement of these discriminatory practices. Others said that even if Tamils were hired today it was extremely difficult for them to stay in the forces, as Sinhala was the only language used, and that, even after selection, Tamils are not promoted according to merit, but are held back and, further, that Tamils feel vulnerable and uncomfortable because they are so outnumbered.

xvi) Relationship between the security forces and the civilian population in Jaffna

As mentioned earlier all reports indicated a great deal of on-going hostility between the armed forces and the civilian population of the northern province.

On the one side General Atygalla said that the soldiers were very defensive and resentful because military personnel were frequently shot at and killed from behind by militants. He described the members of the armed forces as feeling that government regulations did not permit them to fight the militants on equal ground, that they were being murdered in cold blood, and that they were receiving no co-operation from the civilian population in their efforts to find the terrorist leaders. He said that these leaders repeatedly escape to southern India, only twenty miles across the Palk Strait, and later return to renew their fighting. Soldiers can obtain no evidence or assistance to help with their enquiries, even when attacks take place in broad daylight and in front of civilian witnesses. General Atygalla also stated that the terrorists were hidden and protected by the civilian population, thus adding to the frustrations of the soldiers in the north.

Further allegations are that the citizens of Jaffna refuse to co-operate with the soldiers in any way, so that they are not able even to buy produce, growers refusing to sell it to them. Consequently if they need food they have to take it forcibly.

On the other hand we were told by several Tamil lawyers, students and citizens in Jaffna that there was no truth in this last assertion, that the soldiers just took anything they wanted, goats, chickens, etc. and that the civilians did not dare complain to the police for, if they did, there would be reprisals. In addition we were told that in order to avoid depradations of produce by the soldiers small farmers would, for example, harvest their onion crops in the middle of the night. However, this activity also had its dangers, as people out at night were often shot at by military personnel. We were unable to substantiate either of these sets of assertions.

According to many of the people interviewed in Jaffna the armed forces continually harrass the civilian population in and around the city. Examples were given of soldiers travelling along in army vehicles and striking with heavy bars, or throwing sharp stones at, cyclists and pedestrians on the roadside. We spoke to people who had witnessed many such incidents. One agricultural worker was reported to have lost an eye as a result of a sharp stone being hurled at him from a passing army jeep. We were told also that soldiers frequently performed such acts as stopping a youngster on a bicycle, beating him up and then running an army truck over the bicycle.

Rapes by soldiers of local girls and women were said to be not uncommon. Reasons given were the hostility between the military and civilian populations, the lack of social life for the soldiers, and their feelings of estrangement from the local people so that their conduct was not tempered by any feelings of restraint. Since most of the soldiers are Sinhalese and speak only this language, and the population in the north is predominantly Tamil, and speaks Tamil, communication between the two groups is difficult in any event. The armed forces in Jaffna were described as having the attitude of an army in occupation. Families of girls raped are reluctant to report these incidents or to give evidence — partly because the Tamil society in the northern province is a protective one and parents are inhibited by a reluctance to let others know that their daughters have been raped, but also because there is fear of the reprisals which are said frequently to follow any complaint.

As the relationship between the armed forces and the civilian population in Jaffna is so distrustful and uneasy, it seemed unlikely that there would be co-operation with the soldiers in their attempts to deal with the militants. Further, informers have been killed by the guerillas. The people in the north are in fear, both of the armed forces, and of the militants.

In any altercation between civilians and soldiers the soldiers are armed and so have the advantage. Under the emergency regulations possession of a firearm by a civilian is an offence punishable by death (Regulation 36). By the time we were in Sri Lanka, in late August 1983, the army had been withdrawn from the barracks near the centre of the town of Jaffna to other barracks further away, and the tension in the town had eased considerably as a consequence.

xvii) Theories as to the reasons for the violence
The feeling commonly expressed was that the tensions had been built up and the organisers of the violence had capitalised on these feelings for their own ends. There was a consensus of opinion that there was organisation behind what happened, but many differing theories as to where the responsibility for this organisation lay.

There were many accounts of people being transported by lorries (sometimes it was said that state vehicles and army lorries had been used) to different areas, and that the mobs so transported then initiated violence in those areas, inciting others to follow their example. It was alleged by very many people, some eye-witnesses and some repeating information which they believed to be firmly authenticated, that persons known to be active supporters of the UNP (the United National Party which won the 1977 elections and has been in power ever since) were on many occasions leaders in the gangs perpetrating violence.

Throughout, the destruction of Tamil property was the apparent primary aim. The fact that very little looting took place in the very early stages tended to confirm the conviction about the level of organisation involved. It was observed that many of the people in the gangs were extremely poor so that the temptation for them to loot must have been very great, yet, on the whole, this temptation was resisted in the beginning. Also, it was stressed that the order which was apparent in the big gangs indicated that there was considerable organisation behind their activities.

Because the initial perpetrators of the violence were not involved in theft, and because eye-witnesses in many cases are too terrified to make reports, or have been injured or killed, or have fled to other parts, the apprehension and conviction of the instigators is necessarily rendered more difficult.

A coincidence which caused comment was the fact that the violence broke out precisely six years after the government came to power. Under the *1978 Constitution* Parliament and the President hold office for a six year period. Before this period had expired the President had been re-elected, and a referendum, instead of the usual general election, had been held. At the referendum the electorate had approved an extension of the normal six year term of Parliament to a twelve year term. (This is covered in more detail in the sub-section on the background to the state of emergency: Section IIIB i). Many people in Sri Lanka had objected strongly to the holding of this referendum in the place of a general election, protesting that democracy, so highly valued in this country, was being eroded thereby.

The theories put forward by government spokesmen as to the identity of those behind the July outbreak of violence attributed responsibility to the three leftist parties, and to a "foreign hand". In interviews with government officials we were told that members of the three leftist parties, the JVP, (Janata Vimukthi Peramuna), the NSSP (Nava Sama Samaja Party) and the Communist Party had made many statements to the effect that they would not allow the government to carry on for a second term. The President in an address to the nation which he made on August 22nd had this to say on the matter,

"You are aware that this Government came into office on July 23rd, 1977. The elections were on July 21st. The results were on July 22nd, and myself and the members of my Cabinet took their oaths on July 23rd, 1977. We had the Presidential election last year and the people decided at a Referendum that General Elections which were due in August 1983, will not be held but be postponed for six years. Since the results of the Referendum there have been various speeches and actions by members of certain political parties that they would not let this Government function after August 1983.

I draw your attention particularly to a statement made by Mr. Vasudeva Nanayakkara who was a candidate for one of the by-elections in May 1983 to the Eheliyagoda seat. He had said quite specifically there that if he is elected he would use his powers as a Member of Parliament for extra Parliamentary activity, joining hands with the terrorists in the North for this purpose for achieving their objects. He has further stated that he does not stand for democratic elections, but is prepared to join in what he calls "ARAGALAYA", that is riot or a disturbance or a violent movement for the purpose of seeing that elections are held in August 1983, and this Government does not function after that. It is obvious, therefore, on the statements of the Nava Samasamaja Party leader, Mr. Vasudeva Nanayakkara, that from August 1983, they were preparing for some form of violence or disturbances.

We have evidence that, soon after the referendum or during the referendum, a certain group that were called the Naxalite group, were preparing, by inflaming the people's minds, making them violent-minded against the Government, against the President, that they would take some action, in case they returned to office, to destroy the United National Party and others who thought democratically, including those in the Sri Lanka Freedom Party, who were democratically-minded. We have also the conduct of the JVP which is a party which took to arms in 1971, fought the Government of the day, tried to destroy it, took over the Police Stations and almost succeeded in bringing down a lawfully elected Government. I remember I was the Leader of the Opposition at that time in Parliament. I gave the full support of myself and my Party to Mrs. Bandaranaike to defeat any insurrection which sought to overthrow a legally elected Government.

The JVP also made statements and made it clear after they lost the Referendum, they did not even contest some of the by-elections. They made it clear that they are giving up their parliamentary tactics and that they should take to non-parliamentary tactics in order to defeat a Government, which by a referendum extended its period by more than six years. We have therefore reviewed certain political parties in this country, the Communist Party, the Party of Vasudeva Nanayakkara called the Nava Sarrasamaja Party, the Party of Rohana Wijeweera, the JVP — as dedicated not to the democratic way of life, but to a violent way of forming a Government and maintaining it by violence. We have, on the other hand, the United National Party, the Sri Lanka Freedom Party, which are democratic parties."

The President made similar statements in the interview which he granted to this delegation on August 30th.

On the 30th July these 3 parties, the JVP, NSSP and the Sri Lanka Communist Party, were proscribed under the emergency regulations for having committed or being likely to commit, acts "prejudicial to public safety, the maintenance of public order or the maintenance of essential services". Amongst these parties, only the Communist Party had a seat in Parliament. That party held just one seat.

Following the announcement of the proscription of the parties on July 30th, arrests were made under the emergency regulations of a number of their leaders and members. At first these people were reported as being held incommunicado without being given access to either lawyers, or to their relatives. Later reports indicate that some at least of them have been allowed visits by relatives, but that they have still not been given access to lawyers. On 3rd August, it was reported in the international media that the government had arrested 18 people connected with these three parties, accusing them of involvement in the rioting, and that another 13 were being sought and, if found, would face indefinite detention without trial under the emergency regulations.

Also at this time, government statements indicated that the violence had arisen from a foreign inspired plot to overthrow, or at least to seriously undermine, the government's authority. Hinted at was the involvement of a foreign power which was said to be using the Soviet affiliated Communist Party to destroy Sri Lanka's economic developments.

By the time of our departure from Sri Lanka (September lst) no evidence had been made public to substantiate these allegations of the involvement of either the leftist parties or a foreign power in the July violence.

Many non-governmental people who were interviewed, including several lawyers both Sinhalese and Tamil, were of the opinion that, far from being anti-Tamil, the NSSP has been very positive in its attitude towards the Tamils. The leader was said to be pro-Tamil and very many people said that they considered it most unlikely that the NSSP would have done anything which would have caused detriment to the Tamils. Further we were told that both this party and the JVP have, as part of their manifestos, the proposition that the Tamils should have the right of self-determination.

The Communist Party was said to have no stated position on the issue. Mr. Sarath Muttetuwegama, a member of this party, in a speech made in Parliament on August 4th, described the Communist party approach as follows,

"While we concede to the Tamils the right to determine their future, we ourselves do not advocate a separate state in this small country. It is not feasible." (Hansard, August 4th pp.1338, 1339).

Mr Amirthalingam, the leader of the TULF, in his letter to the President of August 10th expressed the following opinion on the identity of the instigators of the violence:

"The Tamil people do not believe that the left parties had any hand in the attack on the Tamil people...This is, in their view, only an attempt to draw a 'red' herring across the trail. The attack on the Tamil people is pure ethnic violence planned well ahead and executed with ruthlessness by forces close to the Government — the same forces that attacked the strikers in July, 1980; attacked Professor Saratchandra and others at the meeting at the Buddhist congress hall and demonstrated before the houses of the judges. These forces include the armed forces for whom Mr Cyril Mathew always holds a brief in Parliament."

(Mr. Cyril Mathew was at the time the Minister of Industries and Scientific Affairs.)

Asked what, in their opinion, was the main cause behind the outbreak of communal riots in July, many people, university staff and students, social workers, members of civil rights movements, lawyers, members of citizens' groups and womens' groups, expressed the view that violence had been used as a means of dealing with problems for several years, and markedly so since the present government came to power. Instances of outbreaks of violence since July 1977 have been listed in publications produced by the Civil Rights Movement of Sri Lanka. We were told during interviews that peaceful picketing is frequently disrupted by gangs, and that these gangs are not brought to account for their actions. A government sponsored trade union, (the JSS, whose president, Mr. Cyril Mathew, was at the time a government minister) was said to have organised strike-breaking violence to disrupt meetings and strikes, and many other meetings were said to have been broken up by hooligans. Complaints to the police about activities such as these have been ineffective. Some people said that the armed forces were influenced in their failure to protect the Tamil people during the July violence by the knowledge that powerful sections of the government would condone this behaviour, and that no disciplinary action would be taken.

Many people interviewed said they were of the opinion that increasing resort to violence as a resolution to problems was becoming an accepted behaviour pattern in Sri Lankan life.

Further, there were said to have been many incidents of racial propaganda and inflammatory speeches made even at the very top levels of government. Concern was frequently expressed about anti-Tamil, pro-Sinhalese and pro-Buddhist statements being made by members of the government. Many felt that these statements had caused a great deal of the racial tension which had built up by the time of the disturbances.

Statements of government ministers made during the month after the disturbances have indicated a clear determination to find and punish the instigators behind the week of violence, no matter who they are. For instance, in Parliament on August 4th, Mr. Gamini Dissanayake, the Minister of Lands and Land Development and Minister of Mahaweli Development, said:

"...investigations are now proceeding. A lot of missing elements are falling into place. When matters like this happen, it is difficult to get the necessary evidence, but have no fear. This Government is going to reveal to this country the entire truth, warts and all even if it means that a part of the blame or the whole blame should come on the Government".

A government publication of September 19th 1983, *Sri Lanka, Beyond Conflict*, contained a clear statement of the government's intention to bring to justice those responsible for the atrocities in July,

"Arresting miscreants who had created Sri Lanka's Violent July, tracing lost goods, and gathering evidence for indictment against suspects has been a round-the-clock occupation of police teams since July 30th. Some four thousand suspects, many of them recidivists are being held."

Ambassador T. Jayokody said, when speaking at the United Nations on August 22nd 1983, that no stone would be left unturned,

"to identify and bring to the courts all persons responsible for killings, violence, destruction and devastation regardless of their status, ideology and political alignments. There will be no exceptions." (Reuter)

In accordance with this stated determination to discover and punish those responsible many people have been imprisoned. The Sri Lanka News Review on August 18th reported that Mr C.T. Jansz, Deputy Commissioner of Prisons, had stated that over 4,000 persons remanded for riot related offences were now in prison custody. However, despite the number so detained, fears were being expressed that most of these persons would never be charged and that, of those who were, very few would be convicted. The feeling seemed to be that violence and injustice had been condoned in the past and there was no reason to expect that this practice would be changed on this occasion.

In view of these apprehensions it would seem to be very desirable that the government does seriously pursue its determination to discover those responsible for the instigation of the violence, to punish them, and to let the general public know that this has been done.

B. The circumstances of displaced persons and their treatment and situation

i) The displaced persons' camps

During the course of the violence many people fled in terror to schools, police stations, Hindu temples, churches and welfare centres. This was a spontaneous reaction. The government then set about organising facilities, and established displaced persons' camps in many of the locations to which the people had fled. Eighteen camps were set up in Colombo, mainly in school buildings. At the time it was the school vacation. Other camps were set up in outlying districts.

"By the 1st of August there were almost 125,000 displaced or affected persons in ... 50 relief camps. In the Relief Camps sited in Colombo there were about 85,000 persons (almost one-third of the city's Tamil population) and the balance of 40,000 sought shelter in the camps outside Colombo." (*Relief and Rehabilitation of Displaced Persons, A Humanitarian Effort in Sri Lanka* p.3)

Under the emergency regulations the post of Commissioner General for Essential Services was created. The function of this office was to ensure the maintenance of essential services and their co-ordination. Mr. Bradman Weerakoon was appointed to the position. In this capacity Mr. Weerakoon was given wide powers over the requisitioning of property, vehicles and personal services (Regulations 8, 9 10 and 10A).

A second function also was assigned to Mr. Weerakoon — that of the co-ordination of the measures to be taken for the care and rehabilitation of persons affected by the disturbances. The powers he enjoyed as Commissioner General for Essential Services made it possible for Mr. Weerakoon to carry out this second function, and it was in this capacity that he and his department became responsible for the situation of those displaced by the July disturbances. Mr. Weerakoon's evident efficiency, organisational ability, integrity and compassion for the victims of the violence set the tone of the organisation of the government's relief and rehabilitation programme.

Mr. Weerakoon told us that the population in each of 18 hastily arranged Colombo camps ranged from 10,000 down to 2,500 persons. The camps established in the out-stations provided refuge for smaller numbers of people.

The organisation of these camps was under Mr. Weerakoon's overall control. He described this organisation as Phase I. To achieve it he appointed an ad hoc team of 5 Secretaries to Ministries. Meetings were held each morning between this Committee and representatives of organisations such as the Sri Lankan Red Cross, Sarvodaya, religious groups of all denominations, citizens' groups and international agencies such as WHO, UNICEF and Redd Barna. At these meetings activities were planned and co-ordinated. People from different government departments, for example the Social Services Department and the Health Department, were made available to assist with the work in the camps.

Security was organised for the protection of the displaced persons. This involved the provision of lighting, guards for sentry duty and co-operation with the armed forces and the police. Trade Unions provided loud-speaker equipment to facilitate general communication.

Food had to be organised. Some camps had cooking facilities, and some had none. The arrangements made for the provision of food had to take account of such factors. The internal organisation of the camps was carried out by the displaced people themselves. They were responsible for such matters as the organisation of sleeping arrangements, the cutting of firewood, and the cooking where this was possible. Water was a big problem. School sanitary facilities were inadequate. New latrines were constructed, and water supplies had to be provided.

We were able to visit one camp in Colombo, at Thurstan College. This is a large school. At the time of our visit in late August, there were over 3,000 displaced persons there. We were told that 68% of these people were of Indian Tamil origin and were very poor. Most of the more wealthy and middle-class people had left the camps by this stage.

As the camps had been established in the context of a national emergency, conditions were, of course, far from ideal. For instance, we saw several classrooms which were being used as dormitories for 45 people in each. However, the camp was well organised. Each person had a sleeping mat, 3 meals a day were provided, and a cup of tea in mid-morning and mid-afternoon. The camp was extremely clean. There were no flies and there was no smell. Temporary toilets had been erected, additional water supplies brought in and security provided.

I was told by Tamil people that Thurstan College was one of the better camps, and that in some camps no water had been provided. As a result terrible stenches were reported and cleanliness was said to be impossible to achieve. According to these reports the only food said to have been provided in some of the camps was tea in the morning and one quarter of a pound of bread for lunch. Time precluded visits to more of the Colombo camps so that we were unable to see for ourselves what the true position was in these places.

We did visit one other camp. This was in the city of Jaffna. The displaced persons there were in a camp which formerly had been occupied by the army. The army at this stage had been withdrawn to two large army camps outside the city. The accommodation in this former army camp was much more spacious and comfortable than that in Thurstan College. Again, most of the people here were of Indian Tamil origin. Those to whom we spoke were too frightened to return to the places from which they had fled.

We were told of other camps forty miles or so from Jaffna, where the conditions were said to be extremely poor, and the facilities totally inadequate. Unfortunately, because of the strictures of time, we were unable to visit these camps. These reports, however, which we heard mainly from eye-witnesses, were consistent and, as far as it was possible to establish their accuracy without making a visit, the reports seemed to have been justified.

All the persons seeking shelter in the camps were Tamils. Many more Tamil people were driven out of their homes but did not flee to the camps. They were instead sheltered by relatives and friends. Many of these friends were Sinhalese families. We heard of no instances of Sinhalese people fleeing to the camps, although many did require shelter with relatives and friends.

ii) Transportation facilities

By August 5th the numbers in the displaced persons' camps began to fall. Some of those who were able to do so began returning to their homes. Families were encouraged to do this, and were given a few small provisions to assist them when they left the camps.

Many of the people in the camps, however, did not feel safe to return to the Sinhalese-dominated areas from which they had fled. By the end of August many people who remained in the camps had returned to their jobs. They were working during the day but returning to the safety of the camps at night. Of the 800 families living in Thurstan College, 400 men were going to work each day and returning at night. The other 400 bread-winners in the camp had been self-employed and it was not so easy for them to start again.

Other displaced people wished to leave the camps and go to Tamil areas to stay with relatives, at least for a time. The government offered to provide transportation for this purpose. Mr. Weerakoon described this as Phase II of the government programme.

Free passage was provided in boats, buses and trains. Many people left the camps by these means for the Tamil-dominated areas in the north and east. Those who wished to travel by air were charged half the cost. The government subsidised the rest of the fare. In the *Sri Lanka News Review* of August 18th it was reported that 22,000 persons had been transported to Jaffna, Batticoloa, Trincomalee and Badulla. Mr.

Weerakoon said that by late August 52,500 people had been provided with transport through governmental arrangements.

These people mainly left the camps to stay with relatives. Since the relatives could not support them unaided for long periods, arrangements were made for the displaced persons to be met on arrival at their destinations by government agents. Provision was made for them to have a meal and to be given access to washing facilities. Each family should then have received two weeks' rations. Tents and roofing sheets were made available so that temporary extensions could be made to houses to provide the necessary additional accommodation.

Arrangements were made to give to the government employees who had left their jobs as a consequence of the disturbances, a three month salary advance. This commenced from the day on which they left. Pensioners who wished to leave Colombo were given their pension payments in advance. Private sector employers were asked to do likewise and to make similar advance payments to their employees.

iii) Success of the measures taken both in the camps and regarding transportation

The measures taken by the government to ameliorate the immediate plight of the displaced persons were very impressive. The organisation set up to deal with the problems was well planned and it was obvious that a great deal of effort had gone into the streamlining of procedures.

People from the government and public service, the voluntary organisations and international agencies whom we met had clearly done a great amount of work to alleviate the problems of the people in the camps. We were able to interview representatives of Redd Barna (Norwegian Save The Children), an international relief organisation, as well as representatives from several local organisations such as the Women's Bureau, which were involved in providing assistance in the camps. All of those to whom we spoke confirmed the above impression which we had received as to the nature of the measures taken.

The experiences of some of the beneficiaries of the assistance, however, testified to the fact that the efforts being made were not always entirely successful. The magnitude, sudden eruption and nature of the problem made it unlikely that it would be otherwise. There were reports of international aid not reaching camps, that some camps in the northern province were receiving little government aid and being run entirely by the local citizens, that camps were inadequate for the need, and that in many cases the facilities were hopelessly poor.

Further, the conditions of some of the boats used in the transportation operation were said to have been quite inadequate. I was told that on some of the boats the toilet facilities were almost non-existent, and that hardly any food or water was provided.

iv) Rehabilitation

Mr. Weerakoon described the rehabilitation of people as Phase III of the programme. Re-establishing the displaced people either in their former homes and jobs, or helping them create a new life-style is, of course, the vital aspect now. To overcome the feelings of insecurity which made people reluctant to return to their earlier places of residence from which they had fled, Mr. Weerakoon's department sought to develop, in the neighbourhoods to which these people would be returning, groups of people willing to become involved with helping them to re-establish themselves and to feel safe. Committees were formed from people in the neighbourhood, and from members of non-governmental organisations, particularly religious groups. These people volunteered to take neighbours from the camps back to their neighbourhood and they assumed responsibility for watching over them.

Many people, of course, had no homes to which they could return. Their places of residence had been destroyed during the disturbances, or the places which they had rented were no longer available to them. After the disturbances many Sinhalese property owners were unwilling to rent accommodation to Tamil people. The wealthier people were able to obtain bank loans to repair or rebuild their properties. REPIA (an organisation set up by the government and described later) was able to assist with the arrangement of long term loans with low interest repayments. For some there was access to a scheme under which, in normal circumstances, a small social service payment is available to anyone who loses his house. Mr. Weerakoon was endeavouring both to obtain an increase to that amount, and also to encourage non-governmental organisations to help these people with grants and practical assistance.

People without secure jobs, and those who had been self-employed, generally needed to be able to return to the neighbourhoods from which they had come in order to re-establish themselves. They were being encouraged to pay a visit to their areas so that they could at least look around and see for themselves that normal life was in fact being re-established.

Those who had left for the Tamil-dominated areas of the country felt more secure. However they had different problems. Generally these people have gone into areas which do not offer the same opportunities for employment and business as were present in the areas from which they had fled. They are unable to stay with relatives indefinitely. Further, great strain is put on the existing facilities in these places. Some of these people will settle eventually on the land in the north, so that settlement schemes will need to be established. The Ministry of Lands has been given responsibility for this.

However, many of the people who have left their original places of residence are not farmers, and do have jobs in Colombo and other centres. It is expected that most of these persons will choose eventually to return to their jobs. Of course some jobs formerly held by Tamils who fled from their original abodes have, in their absence, been given to other people. Consequently, unemployment faces these particular people whether they choose to remain in the north or return to their original place of residence.

The seriousness, and the continuing nature, of the problems of many of the displaced Tamils is illustrated by the following article which appeared in *The Tamil Times* in December 1983, several months after the interviews conducted by the delegation:

"Though several months have elapsed since ethnic violence erupted in Sri Lanka, about 25,000 refugees are still languishing in the 39 state-run camps and an equal number in the unofficial 'welfare centres' scattered throughout the island.

Alagappan's family, like many others, occupies a little tent it has pitched in the Bambalapitiya Hindu College grounds, the biggest of the four state-run camps in Colombo, which accommodates 6,500 men, women and children.

'We are too frightened to return to our homes,' explained Alagappan's daughter Nagamma. 'We want to go to India,' she said. A group of about 25 people who gathered around repeated her proposition in a chorus.

Karuppiah, a barber who escaped death because a Sinhalese gentleman sheltered him from an angry mob, explained his predicament thus: 'I have very high regard for the Sinhalese people. But the thugs are instigated by powerful forces to attack the Tamils. I love this country but I cannot hope to live here. How can we live in the camps for ever? Outside it is not safe,' he said. 'We cannot go back, they are chasing us,' the middle-aged Pandiyan said. 'The landowner has given my vegetable plot to the Sinhalese.'

His wife Lakshmi refuted the charge that they were not leaving the camps because they wanted to enjoy the regular supply of food and clothing. 'What are they giving us? One-third of a loaf of bread and tea in the morning, rice with pumpkin and cabbage for lunch and one-third of a loaf of bread and vegetables for dinner. Can you eat this daily?' she asked. 'We are willing to go back to our plots if they are returned and safety assured,' she said.

Most of the inmates in the camps are stateless persons. They have no place to go. But there are also a few Lankan nationals, especially in the camps in the North and East, the predominantly Tamil areas. They are the refugees who fled from Colombo and other Sinhala areas. They have no house or relatives in the Tamil provinces to accommodate them. Many of them say that their houses in the Sinhala areas were burnt. Sinhala owners are not willing to rent out their houses to them.

Those whose houses were damaged are reluctant to invest money on repairs and those whose houses were completely gutted are in a predicament. They are promised low interest long-term loans. 'It will take months to process the papers. The loan offered is too little, it is not sufficient to build even a hut,' said a dejected Colombo resident who lost his house."

v) Missing persons

A further problem was that, in the confusion and panic, many families had become separated. Attempts were made to trace missing persons. Registers of people were compiled in all the camps, and notes made of those reported missing. These records were then circulated. However, particularly in the early stages, some people were too frightened to give the names and addresses of their missing relatives and friends. They feared that this information might get into the hands of those who had been involved in the earlier acts of violence, and that the infomation might be used to supplement the lists already used by the attackers. By the end of August the attempts made to trace missing persons had not met with much success. At that point a representative of the Red Cross tracing agency arrived in Sri Lanka to assist with the problem.

vi) The Rehabilitation of Property and Industries Authority

An organisation called REPIA (the Rehabilitation of Property and Industries Authority) was set up by the government under the emergency regulations, (Emergency (Rehabilitation of Affected Property, Business or Industries) Regulations, No. 2 of 1983).

The purposes to be fulfilled by REPIA were described as follows by Mr R.G. de Mel, Minister of Finance and Planning:

"(a) the repair and restoration of affected property; (b) the rehabilitation of affected industries and businesses. The objectives of REPIA are: To protect tenants displaced by the riots, to protect house owners from being exploited by unscrupulous tenants or by others, to take responsibility for restoring tenancy rights. To intervene where house owners may be pressurised to sell their properties at depressed prices. To give permission for repairs by owners of owner occupied dwellings subject to normal planning regulations. Where industrialists required financial support, the government would consider the need to acquire shares in such enterprises."

(*Daily News*, Friday August 26th, p. 8.)

In order that it might be able to discharge its functions REPIA was given very wide powers of acquisition of property, wide powers enabling it to organise clearance and re-development, to enter into contracts, powers to control and to manage, and powers to requisition property, vehicles and services (Regulation 5 of the REPIA regulations).

Every property affected by the violence, be it private home or business premises, was automatically vested absolutely in the State free from all encumbrances. (Regulation 9(1)). "Affected property" was defined in Regulation 19 to mean "any immovable property damaged or destroyed on or after July 24th, 1983, by riot or civil commotion and includes any immovable property used for the purpose of an affected business or industry". Under Regulation 9(2) of the REPIA regulations, the decision as to whether or not properties were to be considered to be "affected" was to be made by REPIA. The REPIA decision was to be final and conclusive and not to be called into question.

REPIA has the power, under Regulation 14 of the REPIA Regulations, to divest such property, industry or business should it see fit to do so.

Fears were expressed that some Tamils whose property had been vested in the state under the emergency regulations, would find themselves permanently deprived of their property. This fear seemed particularly prevalent in relation to the smaller Tamil enterprises, and seemed to have been much more widely felt immediately after the regulations establishing REPIA were brought into effect than was the case at a later date. Tamil confidence that the property would be restored seemed to increase as time went on.

In an interview with Rear-Admiral A. Perera, the Chairman of REPIA, and with several of the other officials of REPIA, we were assured that the property is re-vested in its rightful owners as soon as an individual can show he is able to repair it without requiring government assistance. He said that the aim of REPIA is to protect the owners of damaged property from exploitation by unscrupulous persons wishing to take advantage of the situation, to protect them in a time of crisis from manipulation and pressure from those who would otherwise be able to take advantage of their misfortune and their need for liquid funds. He said that the intention was simply to provide a safeguard.

At the time of the interview, in the last week in August, Rear-Admiral Perera told us that title to over 1,000 houses and businesses had already been re-vested in the original owners.

Another important function stressed by REPIA officials was the rebuilding of factories, the re-establishement of businesses, the recovery of jobs lost in the destruction, and the resuscitation of trade and prosperity. The people appointed to REPIA had been entrusted with the task of bringing about the rapid reconstruction of industry and the reduction of unemployment.

Rear-Admiral Perera told us that REPIA was involved in arranging for banks to give long-term low-interest loans to aid in the reconstruction of damaged property. Outright grants tied to a means test were also under consideration.

The fears of some Tamil businessmen were described by Mr. Amirthalingam (leader of the TULF party) in an interview recorded in *The Tamil Times*. Basically Tamils feel that the measures taken require factories and businesses to be rebuilt in the places where they originally stood. Because they fear further attacks many owners would prefer them to be rebuilt elsewhere, often in predominantly Tamil areas.

III

ESCALATING VIOLENCE

Introduction to the second LAWASIA report, June 1985
The situation within Sri Lanka over the past few years is one which has been deteriorating. Even though the current violence, with the exception of the recent brutal and tragic incident in Anuradhapura, has so far been contained within the northern and eastern parts of the island, (the area claimed by the Tamil militants for the separate state which they wish to establish and where Tamils form a high proportion of the population), there is tension and insecurity throughout Sri Lanka, and people and positions are becoming more polarised. The number of acts of violence being committed both by the Tamil militants on the one side, and the almost totally Sinhalese security forces on the other, in which combatants and non-combatants from both Sinhalese and Tamil groups are being killed and injured, is rapidly escalating.

Since I was not able, during my 5 day visit, to travel to the troubled northern part of the island, I am unable to give an updated factual account of the acts of violence which are taking place in those parts. The versions of the events sometimes differ wildly according to the sources of information. Government sources consistently report fewer casualties among the security forces than do Tamil sources, and in many instances accounts are conflicting as to the numbers of unarmed civilians killed, and how and why they were killed, in attacks carried out by both sides.

What is clear is that, until very recently, very few Sinhalese civilians had been attacked by the Tamil militants, despite repeated and frequent atrocities carried out by the security forces upon unarmed Tamils.

What is also clear, and not denied by anyone to whom I spoke, is the serious situation of deprivation and hardship in which the people of parts of the north and east are currently placed. According to reliable reports this situation is rapidly worsening, and is caused mainly by government imposition of extremely stringent emergency regulations, but also in part by the constant disruption to rail and road communications resulting from the attacks of Tamil militants.

If there is to be any hope of re-establishing normal existence within the northern and eastern parts of the country and maintaining a workable relationship between these areas and the rest of the country, there must be immediate de-escalation of the violent measures and both sides must turn to serious negotiation.

The All Party Conference, the negotiations between the government, other political parties and certain prominent organisations and associations, which commenced meetings in January, 1984, in an attempt to find a peaceful solution, collapsed in acrimony, without any agreement having been reached, in December, 1984. (This is covered in more detail in the sub-section dealing with that Conference, IIIB ix).

The clear indications now are that the government has elected to pursue a military solution. When I interviewed the Minister for National Security, Mr. Lalith Athulathmudali, he readily acknowledged that a military solution cannot be the final resolution to the problem, and that ultimately a political solution must be reached, but he also insisted that before any further attempts at negotiation are made the militants must be defeated. On March 28th, 1985, in *The Daily News*, a Colombo newspaper, Mr. Athulathmudali was reported as saying, "We are prepared to forgive the terrorists if they lay down their arms..." The Minister said that everyone spoke of a political solution.

"I, too, say a political solution is necessary at the end. But the terrorists are not interested in a political solution. Therefore, it is like asking a person to clap with one hand. The terrorists believe they could win this war...so long as they believe this they would not stop the violence. Therefore we must convince them that they cannot win it.

Some of them have already been convinced. Only a few leaders and hard core remain to be convinced. We have to convince them too. Then alone they will lay down their arms."

While I was in Sri Lanka the President addressed Parliament on the occasion of its opening on February 20th, 1985. With reference to the government's current approach to the militants, quoting an earlier address he had made to Parliament, he said,

"...I feel that the terrorist campaign has made agreement difficult. I wonder whether they want a solution. Some think that a solution will make terrorism wither away. Others think that any solution will be impossible unless terrorism is first eliminated.

I think the last sentence is correct".

At a later part of the same opening address the President stated,

"The borders of Sri Lanka are Point Pedro and Devinuwara in the North and South; Batticoloa and Colombo in the East and West. The terrorists are attempting to shoot their way into the heart of Sri Lanka to the borders of what they call the State of Eelam. If we do not occupy the Border, the Border will come to us. We intend to act before they succeed.

We have to combat 'terrorism' and defeat it with all the resources at our command. We may have to equip ourselves to do so at the expense of development and social and economic welfare plans. Let us then unitedly decide to do so and as one Nation and one People bend ourselves to this task."

Racial tensions very often increase as the economic circumstances of the people deteriorate. This appears to have happened in Sri Lanka. The country's economic problems are being compounded by the fact that vast amounts of money are being spent on military measures. The President revealed this in the extract quoted above. In the same speech he also said,

"Immense resources needed for the development of our country, for education, research, health and welfare have had to be diverted to provide greater security for civilians everywhere..."

According to a news bulletin broadcast by the Australian Broadcasting Corporation on May 26th, 1985, the Finance Minister, Mr. Ronnie de Mel, has announced that an extra U.S.$72,000,000 will be spent on defence this year. At present the security operations are said to be costing approximately U.S.$600,000 a day. The Minister was reported to have stated that the government was prepared to spend any amount to safeguard the nation's unity.

So far, attempts made by the government to control the problem by strong legislative, administrative and military measures have not worked. In fact they have been counter-productive. They have hardened Tamil resistance and turned many formerly moderate Tamils, who originally were opposed to the idea of a separate state, to the view that separatism is the only way in which to guarantee their physical safety.

It is important to look at the escalation of violence both from the perspective of the government and that of the Tamil minority. It is essential to bear in mind the fact that, within both the Sinhalese and Tamil communities there are many people, still, who have friends within and are pleasantly disposed towards, the other community. In fact, during the massacres of July, 1983, there were many acts of heroism by Sinhalese people, who in many cases risked their own lives to save those of their Tamil friends and neighbours. There is yet opportunity for dialogue between the two groups to be established and to work, but the longer the current situation continues, with its violence, injuries, death and destruction the more difficult it must inevitably become to bridge the widening gaps and the growing resentments between the two communities.

A. Grievances between the two communities and related background factors

There is a history of perceived discrimination in the eyes of both groups, each group seeing the other as having unfair privileges and advantages. Some of these perceptions are due more to misunderstandings and myths than to actual facts. Some have real foundation.

Paul Sieghart, in the report which he wrote for the ICJ after a visit to Sri Lanka in January 1984, refers to a paper prepared by the Marga Institute, (a research institute based in Colombo), entitled "Inter-Racial Equity and National Unity in Sri Lanka." He points out that in this paper it is made clear that there are no statistically significant differences between the Tamil and Sinhalese communities in any of the critical social and economic indicators. Neither group is, in relation to the other, under-privileged with respect to infant mortality rates, standards of nutrition, life expectancy, employment rates, average income of households or ownership of consumer durables.

Nevertheless, some of the peceived grievances do have foundation in fact.

i) The status of Tamils "of recent Indian origin"

One sector of Sri Lankan society with very real cause for feeling aggrieved is that group of people known as "Indian" Tamils, or Tamils "of recent Indian origin". The Tamil population of Sri Lanka consists of two distinct elements. The two communities of Tamils do not mix a great deal, but they share a common feeling of insecurity as minority groups.

The majority of the Tamils in the country are the "Sri Lankan", "Ceylon"or "Jaffna" Tamils. They form 12.6 % of the nation's population. They have lived in Sri Lanka for hundreds, possibly thousands of years. The arrival in the country of both the Sinhalese and Tamils is shrouded in myths and legends, but it seems that members of both groups have been in the island for at least two thousand years. Historically, the Sinhalese have considered the Tamils as invaders upon Sinhalese territory. Both groups originally came to Sri Lanka from India: the Sinhalese from northern, and the Tamils from southern India. Many of the Sri Lankan Tamils live in the northern and eastern parts of the country, but quite a sizeable number of them also live in predominantly Sinhalese areas, and many of these people have spent all their lives in such areas. Generally the Sri Lankan Tamils are reasonably prosperous and well educated.

The Indian Tamils on the other hand are descendants of people brought over to Sri Lanka by the British in the nineteenth century to work firstly on coffee, and later on tea, plantations. They form 5.6 % of the total population. These people still live mainly in the hill country in the central part of the island, and most of them still work on the plantations. By their labour they have contributed enormously to the country's national income. Yet they are a poor and under-privileged sector of the community. They have not participated in the ethnic violence, except to be victims of it. In different incidents of communal disturbances they have been the victims of attacks by sectors of the Sinhalese community, and, on these occasions, the security forces have often failed to provide protection, and in some cases are reported to have participated in the depradations.

In July, 1983, although in no way involved in the call for Eelam, or with the militants, many of the Indian Tamils were affected by the violence in the hill country. For instance Mr. Thondaman, Minister for Plantations and Rural Industries, told me that 3,700 Indian Tamils had been driven from the Divitura Estate and had fled to a displaced persons' camp at Elpitiya, and that 400 of these people had lost everything they owned. Many other plantations were affected as well. Some people from the lower lying plantations in the south fled to camps near Colombo.

In the up-country areas only in isolated instances were the estates themselves attacked, but the towns serving the estates were attacked and the population on the estates was affected by this violence since many children of the estate workers have moved to these towns and now run shops and businesses there.

Further, I was told that Indian Tamil settlers had, from early July 1983 onwards, been driven away from areas to which they had fled after the 1981 riots. In the statement adopted by the National Council of the Ceylon Workers' Congress on August 14th 1983 the position was described thus:

"Even before the riots began in Colombo, the attack on the Tamil settlers in the Mannar, Vavuniya and Trincomalee areas had been set in motion. It is significant that communal violence on a large scale commenced with the burning of the huts of settlers in Trincomalee. They were uprooted from their homes in the early hours of the morning of 24th July, bundled and brought against their will to Nuwara Eliya and Hatton and left as destitutes.

The failure of the Minister of Lands and Land Development to give shape and content to a decision of the Cabinet to regularise the land holdings of stateless persons and other people of Indian origin in the North through a dialogue with the Minister of Rural Industrial Development and the President of the Ceylon Workers Congress has been a major contributory factor to this sad state of affairs which we are witnessing today.

Instead of implementing the declared policy of regularising the settlements of persons of Indian origin in these areas, where they were transported and dumped as refugees after the previous holocausts, a concerted attempt had been made by the officials to drive them out of their holdings under various false pretexts. This had been further intensified around the middle of July when the police and security personnel set in motion a wave of terror intimidating the settlers and driving them away.

In order to legalise this programme, the Minister of Lands and Land Development has submitted a proposal 'For Prevention of encroachments and illicit settlements in Sri Lanka, the Prevention of unlawful activities of any individual, group of individuals, Associations, Organisations or body of persons within Sri Lanka...' which gives wide powers to the Minister and includes some of the obnoxious provisions of the Prevention of Terrorism Act, like detention without trial by order of the Minister of Lands for up to 18 months, power to Government Agent or Assistant Government Agent, without going to Courts to authorise police, army or navy to demolish buildings etc., thus branding settlers as terrorists.

It is also significant that while the proposal of the Minister of Lands and Land Development is still under consideration by the Government, the Minister had instructed the Government Agents to take action as if the law is already in force."

In August 1983 I was able to speak to some Indian Tamils in displaced persons' camps both in Colombo and in Jaffna. Their fear of returning to the plantations from which they had fled was evident. Many expressed a desire to go to India. However, many of these people are stateless and this solution seemed one not likely to be offered to them.

I was told by several people who were working to assist the Indian Tamils that the plantation workers no longer have any confidence in the security forces, that when these workers were attacked some of the superintendants of the plantations stood by, as did army personnel when present, and that sometimes there was active co-operation by these persons in the violence. The general feeling of the Indian Tamils whom I met in the camps seemed to be one of fear, helplessness and despair.

From the evidence it appears that until very recently virtually no members of the Indian Tamil community had joined the militant Tamil groups. Even in 1985, as far as I could ascertain, very few Indian Tamils were thought to participate in militant activities.

Although born in, and, in many cases, descended from one, two or more generations of ancestors also born in Sri Lanka, large numbers of these people do not now have Sri Lankan citizenship and are effectively stateless persons. Because they do not have citizenship they cannot vote. This situation carries with it many concomitant disadvantages. Such a powerless group has difficulty in securing equal treatment for itself and suffers from disadvantages in many aspects of life as a result. For instance, services such as the education and medical facilities provided in the areas where Indian Tamils reside have been of a very low standard and, in matters such as social welfare benefits and the granting of cost of living adjustments, the provisions for these people lag seriously behind those enjoyed by other sectors of the community.

Their situation was described recently as follows:

"the plantation workers have been consistently denied wage increases, educational, medical, social and welfare benefits extended to other sectors of the population which is once again a blatant act of discrimination. In this context the granting of citizenship alone is insufficient."

(Statement Adopted by the National Council of The Ceylon Workers'
Congress, August 14, 1983, p.2)

Prior to Independence the Indian Tamils, in common with all others
born in either India or Sri Lanka, were British subjects and were entitled
to vote. In the general elections of 1947 they had elected 7 Indian Tamil
Members of Parliament and had exercised a significant influence on the
voting in other electorates also.

The *1948 Constitution* contained no provisions concerning citizenship.
This turned out to be a very grave omission.

One of the first acts of the new government was to determine the
citizenship requirements of the country. In 1948 legislation was enacted
conferring citizenship only on those people who had either been born
in Sri Lanka to fathers also born there or, if the persons seeking
citizenship had not been born in the island, their fathers and
grandfathers must have been born there. Due to the lack of records
such facts were very difficult to prove. Although not all people were
required to furnish the specified proof in order to acquire citizenship,
the Indian Tamils were required to provide it, and were generally unable
to do so.

A second law made citizenship available by registration in certain
circumstances, but, for various reasons, very few Indian Tamils took
advantage of this provision. As a result most of the Indian Tamils were
rendered effectively stateless and, as a consequence, were
disenfranchised as well.

Article 15 of the *Universal Declaration of Human Rights* declares that
"Everyone has the right to a nationality". The situation which occurred
in 1948 amounted to an entirely arbitrary refusal of the basic right to
the citizenship of their own country to people who, for the most part,
had never lived anywhere else and who, by their labour, had contributed
enormously to their nation. Unfortunately, at the time, even the Sri
Lankan Tamil community did not raise its voice in an attempt to remedy
this obvious injustice.

In 1964 an agreement was reached with India by which a certain
number of Indian Tamils were to be given Indian citizenship and to go
to that country to live. The rest were to be granted Sri Lankan
citizenship. As yet this agreement, although partially implemented, has
not been implemented in full. Consequently, to this day, many Tamils
"of recent Indian origin" living and working in the plantations in the
hill country are without citizenship in Sri Lanka.

It is urged that this situation be given immediate attention, that
legislation be passed to confer Sri Lankan citizenship upon all those
who do not voluntarily leave the country for India under agreements
made to this end, and that the disparity of treatment accorded to these

people in other respects be remedied also. Such a step is essential if the obvious inequities here are to be removed.

Welcome recommendations to this effect were made at the 1984 All Party Conference by its "B" Committee. (The All Party Conference is considered more fully in the sub-section devoted to that topic, Section IIIB ix). The "B" Committee recommended that, with repect to education, special concessions be given to disadvantaged groups like the Tamils of recent Indian origin on the grounds of economic and social factors. It was noted that the former plantation schools had now been taken over as government schools. However, it was pointed out that, owing to very long years of gross neglect, their facilities, teaching staff and programmes of instruction are extremely poor. Already some programmes are reported to have been commenced to rectify this situation, and it was recommended that every effort should be made to integrate the schools of the plantation areas with the rest of the national education system. This, in turn, would require certain necessary inputs to raise the schools to the national level. It is to be hoped that these recommendations will be implemented without delay.

In relation to the problem of statelessness, the President, on September 21st, 1984, in his report to the All Party Conference said that there was no opposition expressed to the proposal that those Tamils of recent Indian origin who did not return to India under the provisions of the 1964 agreements should be given Sri Lankan citizenship. The number of such persons was estimated at around 90,000. Some people gave me much higher estimates. Whatever the accurate number of persons involved, it is urged that these recommendations be speedily fulfilled, so that this particular and very clear injustice be terminated.

[Note: Since this section was written I understand that the government has passed legislation which, if implemented, should confer citizenship on at least some of the Indian Tamils who were stateless at the time of the writing of this report.]

ii) University education and state sector employment

Since Independence in 1948 Tamils have been, and continue to feel, discriminated against both under the university admission system, and by the hiring policies adopted by successive governments in relation to employment within the government service and state-owned corporations.

The discriminations which favour Sinhalese people have been seen by the governments practising them as necessary in order that the situation which had prevailed in colonial times might be reversed. During those times Tamils held what was perceived to be a disproportionately large number of university places and high governmental positions and dominated the professions. This happened partly because particularly good missionary schools had been established in Tamil areas, and partly as a consequence of other factors which have motivated Tamils in Sri Lanka to view education as the means to economic progress, hence to work hard at education and to do very well. Since this is the case, from a Tamil point of view, accessibility to university places upon a criterion of merit is extremely important.

The measures taken to significantly increase the numbers of Sinhalese in universities and in public sector employment included the provision of better schools in Sinhala districts, a government policy favouring Sinhalese in recruitment to state jobs, and "standardisation" and then "quota" systems of admissions to universities. These measures have greatly reduced the proportion of places in these institutions gained by Tamils.

Today university admission is based on a quota system. Only 30% of the university places are awarded on merit; 15% go to areas declared to be disadvantaged, and the remaining 55% to areas according to the quota system. This has the result that students from one region who have higher marks than those obtained by students in another may nevertheless find those from the latter region, with the lower results, being awarded the available university places. Tamil people feel that this quota system operates very unfairly against them and that it is discriminatory.

Statistics compiled by the Marga Institute, a research organisation based in Colombo, show that out of the university admissions in 1983, 75% of the places went to Sinhalese, and 19.3% to Tamil students, and that, in 1981, the literacy rate amongst Sinhalese was 88.4% and amongst Tamils was 86.6%. (See *Far Eastern Economic Review*, Nov.17, 1983, p.31. The Tamils mentioned include both those of Sri Lankan and Indian Tamil origin.)

Statistics released by the Division of Planning and Research, University Grants Commission 1983, are given on the following page.

Since the previous imbalance would thus appear to have been corrected, there seems to be no longer any need to compensate for the earlier inferior education facilities available to the Sinhalese. The education provided in Sinhalese areas has now been greatly improved.

It would seem that the Tamil grievance regarding university education could be removed quite simply if university places were awarded solely on merit. If 15% of the regions are definitely disadvantaged then provision could be made, within an overall merit system, to give preferential treatment to these few regions until the imbalance that they have suffered is rectified.

The other, related area of grievance here is that, for quite a few years, government policy has been to favour the Sinhalese as against the Tamils in new recruitment to state jobs. Though it is true that many high government service positions are still held by Tamils, for the most part these are people who were hired many years ago.

UNIVERSITY ADMISSION FIGURES

	1981			1982			1983		
	S	T %	O	S	T %	O	S	T %	O
Arts	82.8	13.3	3.9	79.4	16.3	4.3	77.1	16.4	6.6
Physical Science	63.5	31.8	4.7	61.1	33.5	5.5	73.4	23.1	3.6
Biological Science	72.5	24.3	3.2	71.7	26.1	2.2	70.3	23.1	3.6
Engineering	67.2	28.1	4.7	66.9	28.5	4.5	66.4	28.1	5.5
Medicine	72.7	23.1	4.3	72.4	25.3	2.3	72.8	22.1	5.1
Law	73.0	16.2	10.0	68.8	24.0	7.3	78.5	11.5	10.0
Total	76.4	19.2	4.4	74.3	22.0	3.9	75.0	19.3	5.7

Source: Division of Planning and Research University Grant Commission 1983, (Please note that due to rounding of figures the percentages do not always add up to 100).

(*Lanka Guardian*, November 1, 1983, p.10)

The following statistics on public sector employment have been compiled by the Marga Institute: of available government jobs, in 1980 84.3% went to Sinhalese, 11.6% to Tamils; of available jobs in state corporations in 1980, 85.7% went to Sinhalese and 10.6% to Tamils.

The latest figures from the Census of Public and Corporation Sector Employment, compiled in 1980 by the Department of Census and Statistics and Ministry of Plan Implementation are as follows:

State Sector Employment (excluding Corporation Sector), professional and technical, 82% Sinhalese, 12% Tamils, 6% Others; administrative and managerial, 81% Sinhalese, 16% Tamils, 3% Others; all categories, 84% Sinhalese, 12% Tamils, 4% others;

Public Sector Employment, professional and technical, 82% Sinhalese, 13% Tamils, 5% Others; administrative and managerial, 83% Sinhalese, 14% Tamils, 3% Others; all categories, 85% Sinhalese, 11% Tamils, 4% Others.

(See Sri Lanka's Ethnic Problems: Myths and Realities, Committee for Rational Development, *The Lanka Guardian*. November 1, 1983).

As already noted, the population in Sri Lanka is 74% Sinhalese, 18.2% Tamils (Sri Lankan and Indian), 7.1% Muslims and 0.7% Others. (1981 Census Figures). Again, the previous imbalance would seem to have been corrected. Since government employment has been such a traditional career for Tamil people, the above hiring policy has been, and still is, a very real grievance. This grievance would be completely removed if recruitment were made according to merit. Some Tamil people interviewed went so far as to say that if this approach were taken in relation to both government jobs and university admissions, the communal problems would be over. Whether or not that is too hopeful a prognosis, these matters are extremely significant.

In 1984 a committee of the All Party Conference was appointed to consider, *inter alia*, the vexed question of entry to universities. This committee agreed that merit was the best criterion and should be the ultimate aim. However, it pointed to the disparities presently existing in the educational facilities within different schools, some of which are severely disadvantaged in comparison to others even within the same school district. In light of this discrepancy, and until it has been rectified, the committee recommended that, as a temporary measure:

a) schools should be graded into categories according to the facilities available;

b) suitable weighting should be given to the disadvantaged schools; and

c) special concessions should be given to disadvantaged groups like Tamils of recent Indian origin on the grounds of economic and social factors.

It is urged that the ultimate aim, that of the use of merit as the criterion for entry to universities, be moved to immediately.

The same committee also considered the question of equalisation of opportunities in employment, and looked at whether employment within the state sector should be on the criterion of merit alone or on merit within ethnic proportions. Here no consensus was reached. The All Ceylon Muslim League, the Council of Muslims, the Sinhala Associations, the Sri Lanka Buddhist Congress and the DWC (Democratic Workers' Congress) were in favour of maintaining ethnic proportions, whilst the LSSP (Lanka Sama Samaja Party), the Christian organisations and the Hindu organisations were emphatically against recruitment on any form of ethnic basis. Legal advisers pointed out that rigid and fixed ethnic proportions were inconsistent with both international human rights norms and with Article 12(2) of the Constitution. Article 12(2) states that,

"No citizen shall be discriminated against on the grounds of race, religion, language, caste, sex, political opinion, place of birth or any one of such grounds..."

It is urged that the applications of all persons, both for admission to universities and to state sector employment, be considered on the criterion of merit alone without reference to ethnic origin. In this way greater harmony and unity could be promoted. All applicants would be treated as equals, as Sri Lankans, and the perpetuation of distinctions and differences for reasons of race can begin to be dismantled. In addition, two very real grievances of the Tamil population would be removed.

iii) Problems caused by the existence of two major languages

During British rule the medium of education in many schools, especially those in the cities, was the English language. This meant that both races could be, and were, educated together, and provided an essential medium through which friendships which transcended ethnic barriers could be formed. Today, children are taught either in Sinhala, or in Tamil. They grow up separately, speaking different languages, they learn from different basic texts and are imbued with different traditions and cultures. In February 1985 I was told that so many Tamil teachers have now left the mixed Sinhalese-Tamil areas, and particularly the Indian Tamil areas, after recent episodes of communal violence that this has forced the discontinuation of Tamil streams in many of these schools.

Some Sinhalese and some Tamil people speak English in addition to their own language. However, many Sinhalese people do not speak Tamil, and vice versa. Hence many of those who do not speak English, and these people comprise a large proportion of the population, are unable to communicate with each other.

This situation undoubtedly has been instrumental in providing fertile ground for the growing misunderstandings and misperceptions between the two communities. Referring to this state of affairs, Mr. R.J.G. de Mel, Minister of Finance and Planning, said in Parliament on August 4th, 1983,

"I thought that this was one of the last chances we had to solve this problem in a state of friendship with the leaders of the Tamil community, because we happened to know them. We...were in university together. We could at all times communicate with each other. We were friends in those days and remain friends even now on a personal level. But we knew that this would apply only to our generation. Our children did not know each other."

The possibility of improving the opportunities for learning the English language and using that language as a link language was considered at the 1984 All Party Conference. It was stated that,

"improving, expanding and intensifying the teaching of English, by whatever modes, contributes towards the promotion of intercommunal harmony and understanding because at present it is the only link language between the two major ethnic groups. However, any undue concentration of the plums of education to those who do well in English can place the child from the non-English speaking home, and this is the vast majority, at an insurmountable handicap ..."

Bearing this in mind the committee recommended, *inter alia*, that the existing legal requirements that English be taught compulsorily as a second language to all children from the third year in school upwards be properly implemented, and that the teaching of English to all students in universities be improved.

The Committee also considered the possibility of teaching Sinhala and Tamil for use as link languages. Foreshadowed difficulties included the problem of motivating children to learn a new language with a new alphabet, when the similar effort required to learn English would appear to yield much greater benefits in later life. Also, initially a large expenditure on resources would be necessary. Despite these problems, it was recommended that steps should be taken to teach Sinhala to Tamil children and Tamil to Sinhala children from the primary level. It was felt that such an approach could have a great impact upon the promotion of inter-communal harmony.

iv) The status of the Tamil language
Apart from the difficulties caused by the existence of two major languages within the country, the status of the Tamil language within Sri Lanka has been one of the major background grievances underlying the present tensions. The language policies of succeeding Sinhala-dominated governments have been felt by the Tamil people to be an indication of their inferior status, of second-class citizenship.

In 1956, eight years after Independence, Mr. Bandaranaike's government enacted the *Official Language Act*. This legislation provided that henceforth Sri Lanka's only "official" language would be Sinhala. This reversed the resolution, adopted in 1944 by the State Council, that both Sinhalese and Tamil be the official languages of the country. Henceforth the official administration of the country would be conducted in Sinhalese, and proficiency in Sinhalese became a requirement for confirmation of appointment to, and promotion within, the public service.

Two years later, *The Tamil Language (Social Provisions) Act* was passed. This legislation would have ameliorated the situation somewhat, providing as it did for the use of Tamil in the spheres of education, public examinations and official correspondence conducted with Tamil speaking people. Unfortunately, the regulations required for the implementation of this legislation were not brought into effect until 1968 when Mr. Dudley Senanayake implemented the Act in pursuance of an agreement he had reached with Tamil leaders under the 1965 *Senanayake-Chelvanayakam Pact*. He did this amidst strong protests from the opposition parties.

In 1961 Mrs. Bandaranaike's government passed *The Language of the Courts Act*. This Act provided for the replacement of English by Sinhala in certain courts of law. Under this same government the position of

Sinhala as the country's only "official" language was in 1972 given constitutional status.

The present government has sought, by provisions which it included in its *1978 Constitution*, to grant a greater measure of recognition to the Tamil language. Although Sinhala remains the "official" language, and is to "be the language of administration throughout Sri Lanka", both Tamil and Sinhala are declared to be "national" languages. The Constitution provides that both languages may be used in Parliament. English is also used in Parliament, Hansard is published in all three languages. Official documents and laws must be published in both Sinhala and Tamil (Articles 22 and 23).

Today, candidates at any official examination are entitled to be examined, and students are entitled to education, in either of the two official languages. However, there is still discrimination in that candidates for an official examination may also be required to have a sufficient knowledge of the official language (Sinhala), or to acquire such knowledge within a reasonable time after admission to the government service, where such knowledge is reasonably necessary for the discharge of duties (Article 22), but the converse does not apply.

The Tamil language is required to be used in addition to Sinhala as the language of administration in the northern and eastern provinces (Article 22(1)), and any person is entitled to "receive communications from, and to communicate and transact business with, any official in his official capacity, in either of the national languages". (Article 22(2)).

The constitutional protection thus given to the Tamil language was a most welcome step, and a very fair recognition of the rights of an 18% minority. Unfortunately, however, the failure has been in its implementation. Sinhala is still frequently used as the language of communication by government departments even when entirely inappropriate, for instance in replies to letters written in Tamil by Tamil people.

In mid-1983 President Jayewardene ordered special Tamil units to be set up in every Ministry to provide translations, so that letters addressed to Tamil speaking people would henceforth be written in the Tamil language. At the time of my visit in February, 1985, Tamils were still receiving official communications in Sinhalese, and complaining that, despite frequent requests for translations into Tamil or even into English, these translations were not forthcoming.

In August, 1984, the Sub-Committee of Ministers on the Tamil Language, which had been appointed at the All Party Conference, unanimously recommended that, in keeping with Section 22(1) of the *Constitution*, the Tamil language should be used, along with Sinhalese, as the language of adminstration of the Ampara district in the eastern province. It also recommended that a separate department be established and charged with the implementation of the constitutional language provisions, and that special units be established in each Ministry to ensure that this be done. The Sub-Committee noted two shortcomings regarding the present use of language in the courts. The first concerned the shortage of essential staff who could translate and interpret, and the second concerned the lack of equipment such as Tamil typewriters. Speedy correction of these omissions was recommended.

These recommendations are to be welcomed, and now that they have been made, it is urged that their implementation be both swift and thorough.

v) Colonisation

Another major factor which has caused severe problems and resentments is the policy, carried out by successive governments over a long period of time, which relates to land distribution and colonisation. This process began when the British in the nineteenth century brought Tamils from India, the "Indian" Tamils, to work on the plantations. These people were placed on land taken by the British from Sinhalese people in the hill country, to the deep resentment of the Sinhalese there, who had to witness the installation of a new Tamil population in their stead.

More recently, from the 1930s onwards, successive Sinhalese-dominated governments have adopted a policy of colonisation or settlement of the north central and eastern regions of the island, as formerly dry areas are rendered fertile by new irrigation schemes. This colonisation plan has resulted mainly in the re-settling of Sinhalese people from the more densely populated southern areas.

From the outset the Tamil people have objected to the programme where it affects land within the regions which they regard as their traditional homelands. Tamils see the relocation of large numbers of Sinhalese from the south into the areas where Tamils have formed a high proportion of the population, as a deliberate plan to change the ethnic composition of those areas. Among other consequences this type of resettlement inevitably has had the result of reducing the effectiveness of Tamil voting power within the regions.

Some Sinhalese, on the other hand, see the Tamil protest as evidence of what they view as the inflated demands which this group makes. They perceive the underlying motive as being the desire of a minority group to secure for itself large tracts of hitherto sparsely occupied land.

The government approach is that Sri Lanka is home to all Sri Lankans, that all should be free to live in any part of the island, and that the colonisation programmes give due recognition to the rights of all in that under them people are re-settled in numbers proportionate to the ethnic composition of the entire island. As far as I could ascertain there are no statistics available from which it is possible to verify the actual numbers and ethnic proportions of those who have been re-settled under the schemes.

The problem has been a source of agitation for many years, and a means for its resolution was included in the *Bandaranaike-Chelvanayakam Pact*, reached between the government and Tamil leaders in 1957. This Pact provided *inter alia* for the establishment of regional councils and specified the powers which these councils would have. Amongst the powers conferred was control over land distribution. However, that Pact, and the later 1965 Senanayake-Chelvanayakam Pact, which also contained agreement for the creation of regional councils which may have been able to resolve the dispute, were both abandoned unilaterally by the governments of the day due to the pressure mounted against their implementation by the opposition parties of the time. In the first case the UNP (the United National Party, the party currently in power) mounted the opposition. The present President was prominent in the campaign against the implementation of the agreement. In the second case the opposition was spear-headed by the SLFP (the Sri Lanka Freedom Party) and other opposition parties.

The colonisation programmes continue today, and are currently a source of great hostility and tension. Early this year (1985) it was reported that the government had decided to settle 200,000 people in the north and east, in numbers reflecting the country's ethnic proportions. A report in *The Sun*, a Colombo newspaper, of January 19th, 1985, gives this account of the views of the Minister for National Security, Mr. Lalith Athulathmudali, on the plan,

"The 'human principle' behind this national integration programme was 'to hug those who are angry with you and send away those who are friendly with you...'

The Minister said the government was considering training the settlers in defending themselves.

'I believe this is the most successful method of combatting terrorism in a non-violent way ... This could mean that somewhere in the future there could be more Sinhalese in the north than Tamils...'

Mr. Athulathmudali said the government had also given the option for those in the north to settle in the south.

'We have assured them of their safety and many of them have now realised that it is much safer for them in the south than in Jaffna'.

He said the programme was one of many options being considered by the government in alleviating the problems of all citizens of the country. 'We are a multi-ethnic, multi-religious country and we must look at the problems of all, not just one section'".

In *The Daily News*, March 28, 1985, the following report appeared,

"Mr. Athulathmudali said that when 200,000 persons are settled in the Vanni the terrorists would have to look sharp. Terrorists should know that the government was determined and dead serious about it...."

In *The Daily News*, of Saturday April 20th, 1985, Mr. Athulathmudali was reported to have said that the settlers would come "from all communities committed to uphold the sovereignty and the unitary state of Sri Lanka", that the recruits would be not only farmers but also soldiers who would live in friendship with other communities. He added that all recruits to the new camps would be given a thorough training in the use of arms and modern agricultural technology.

The proposed implementation of this programme at this time must be viewed as alarming. It may be that, in some situations, a policy of settling a large number of Sinhalese amongst Tamils would have great merit. However that may be, at present, in the current climate of suspicion and distrust, an inevitable result of moving people of one ethnic group from one part of the island to a different part of the island considered by the other major group to be its traditional land, taking some of that land and giving it to these new and different settlers, who are not always farmers, would seem guaranteed to escalate the incidents of violence even further.

In view of the mounting hostilities and tensions in these regions, as is indicated in the above newspaper reports, the Sinhalese settlers are being trained in tactics of self-defence for their own protection and it seems that some have been provided with arms.

The dangers inherent in such a situation are too obvious to be ignored, and it is urged that this policy be reviewed. It is recommended that, as an immediate measure, the colonisation of areas regarded by Tamils as their traditional homelands be discontinued.

vi) Decentralisation

There can be no doubt that the call for separation has played a very large part in the escalation of communal hostilities in the country. However, it would seem that until very recently only a very small minority of Tamils supported the idea of a separate state.

Most Sri Lankans, whether Tamils, Sinhalese or Muslims, have been of the opinion that the concept of a separate state in such a small country is not a viable one.

A former Chief Justice of Sri Lanka, The Honourable M.C. Sansoni, summed up his assessment of the situation in the following words:

"Nothing was further from the minds of the people of Sri Lanka throughout its history than a division of the country, under which a separate area or areas will belong to a particular racial or language group. There has always been freedom of movement from any part of the country to another, for every inhabitant treated it as his own as well as everyone else's and was proud to belong to it and to own it. All races and religions regarded the entire island as their common home, for no part of it was separately owned by any group. Anybody was free to settle and live undisturbed anywhere, and to exercise and enjoy all the rights of a citizen to the fullest extent. The establishment of a separate State to be owned and governed by any particular group of the people will affect and diminish the rights, powers and privileges which are already vested in the entire population. It cannot be permitted, and it will be strenuously resisted, unless the entire nation gives its consent to such a change. Such consent will, if I have correctly read the mood and the temper of the nation, never be given, and any attempt to establish a separate State will inevitably result in civil war and endless bloodshed."

(Report of Presidential Commission of Inquiry into The Incidents which took place between 13th August and 15th September 1977 — Sessional Paper of the Sri Lankan Parliament No. VII, 1980, p.61.)

The overwhelming majority of Tamils within Sri Lanka did not support the idea of a separate state before the disturbances broke out in July 1983. However, understandably, as communal violence continues, more and more Tamils are moving towards regarding separatism as the only way of preserving their lives and those of their families, their livelihood and their homes and possessions.

For the first thirty years after Independence Tamils sought a federal arrangement within one united country, not a separate state. Continued demands for such an arrangement led to provision within both the 1957 and 1965 Pacts for the setting up of regional councils. However, as noted above, these Pacts were never implemented.

One possible solution, canvassed over a long period, and, in the past, favoured by many Tamils, is a form of decentralisation which would give autonomy to local regions, and satisfy Tamil demands for some real control over their destiny in areas where they form a majority of the population.

In 1980, the present government, acting on promises made in its 1977 election manifesto to take steps to remedy Tamil grievances, did set up District Development Councils with the stated aim of achieving decentralisation. This was a welcome step. Unfortunately, inadequate implementation of the scheme has meant that no real devolution of power has occurred. In 1983 a government agent described the Councils to me in the following terms — they have no funding, they have no powers, and, more important, the scheme is not one of devolution, rather what has been done is to bring all the village councils to a central spot. He saw the District Councils as having subsumed two tiers of a four-tier system which, formerly, was very much more accessible to the public. This system consisted of town and village councils which have been absorbed into the District Councils, and urban and municipal councils.

Undoubtedly, the early granting of real autonomy to the different regions in the country would have made it likely that a great deal of the present ethnic tensions could have been avoided. Even now, this policy may still provide an important and viable measure, but real devolution of power must be forthcoming. Under the existing system the District

Ministers and Government Agents are responsible to the central government, and are not agents of the district. This focus on the centre must be altered before the District Councils can effectively bring about decentralisation.

The TULF has supported the move for a separate state and has done so because of a feeling that no other solution is possible if Tamil lives, language, culture and property are to be preserved. However, TULF leaders have made it clear that, despite this position, they are willing to negotiate and to consider any reasonable alternative solution which can be suggested. On the other hand, the militant groups of Tamil youth are now declaring that separation is the only acceptable solution. (The progress of the discussions on regional autonomy which were carried out during the 1984 sessions of the All Party Conference are considered in the sub-section which deals with that Conference (IIIB ix)).

vii) The Demand for 50:50
Although not exactly a grievance, this is part of the background to the present problems and therefore its recording in this section is appropriate. It seems to have been responsible for generating in the minds of a fair number of the Sinhalese community the idea that the Tamil minority in Sri Lanka is always demanding far more than would seem reasonable in relation to its numbers.

The 50:50 demand was made by a Tamil leader, Mr. G.G. Ponnambalam, prior to Independence. It was a demand for parity of representation in the Legislature for all the minorities on the one hand, with the Sinhalese people on the other. It was made because the Tamils realised that self-government would mean that the Sinhalese would play the dominant role in the country. During the eleven years preceding Independence, Tamils had very little participation in the higher levels of government, and they were fearful that this situation would continue.

A State Council was established soon after universal suffrage and internal self-government were achieved in 1931. In the first Council, which existed from 1931 to 1936, Tamils, as well as Sinhalese, were among the chairmen of the Executive Committee, and were represented in the Cabinet. However, from 1936 until the general elections in 1947, all the Executive Chairmen were Sinhalese, and, during this time only one Tamil Cabinet Minister was appointed, Mr. A. Mahadeva in 1942.

It was in this context that the 50:50 demand was articulated. It was never realised. The Sinhalese made some counter-proposals. However, the Tamil leaders of the time were offered participation in the government of the day. They accepted this and the negotiations on the 50:50 demand never reached any concrete conclusion.

viii) The 1948, 1972 and 1978 Constitutions
The *Soulbury Constitution*, the Order-in-Council of the British

Parliament under which Sri Lanka came to independence in 1948, did not contain the protections for which the Tamil minority had hoped but it did contain, in Section 29, provisions which protected the rights of the minorities. Section 29 provided,

"No ... law shall ... make persons of any community or religion liable to disabilities or restrictions to which persons of other communities or religions are not made liable; or ... confer on persons or on any community or religion any privilege or advantage which is not conferred on persons of other communities or religions."

Should any legislation be enacted which was alleged to contravene the rights guaranteed by the *Constitution* the matter could be taken to the courts, and ultimately to the Privy Council in London, which was at that time the final court of appeal in the Sri Lankan court hierarchy.

Despite Section 29, in 1948 the Indian Tamils were deprived of citizenship and disenfranchised. In 1956 the *Official Languages Act* was enacted providing that Sinhala henceforth would be the only official language, and systems have been adopted which favoured Sinhalese students in their applications for admission to universities, and favoured Sinhalese applicants for jobs in the government sector. (All of these matters have been considered in more detail in the sub-sections concerned with university education and languages (IIIA ii, iii).

Section 29, the safeguards it provided, and appeals to the Privy Council, were abolished when Sri Lanka became a Republic and a new *Constitution* was enacted by Mrs. Bandaranaike's government in 1972. This *Constitution* was not enacted in accordance with the provisions for amendment contained in the 1948 Order-in-Council. The guarantees of minority rights contained in the *1948 Constitution* were not re-iterated in the *1972 Constitution*. Constitutional status was given to the position of Sinhala as the country's only "official" language, and "foremost place" among religions was given to Buddhism. Thus priority status was conferred upon both the language and the religion of the majority Sinhalese community.

As already mentioned the next *Constitution*, promulgated by the present government in 1978, did accord to the Tamil language the status of being a "national" language, though Sinhala is still the only "official" language. Freedom of religion is guaranteed by Articles 10 and 14(c), however, Buddhism remains in the "foremost place" among religions, and Article 9 states that "it shall be the duty of the state to protect and foster the Buddha *Sasana*".

This *Constitution* was promulgated by the present government almost immediately upon gaining office. The TULF refused to participate in either its drafting or adoption. The TULF demanded that an All Party Conference to consider Tamil grievances be held first. The holding of such a Conference had been promised by the UNP in its election manifesto. The Conference was not called at that time, nor for several years later. In fact, as is discussed elsewhere, it was not called until mid-July 1983. Accordingly the new *Constitution* was adopted without the participation of the TULF.

The Tamils have not participated in the drafting, nor in the adoption, of the post-Independence *Constitutions*, and they have put forward the claim that they have, therefore, never relinquished sovereignty over their traditional homelands. They assert that this sovereignty reverted to them when Sri Lanka finally emerged from colonial dependence upon the granting of Independence by Britain in 1948. In essence the Tamils claim the right to the international legal principle of self-determination. It is beyond the scope of this report to do more than simply note the existence of this argument, and that it is used by the Tamil people to support, *inter alia*, their claim to a right to a separate state.

ix) The identification of Buddhism with Sinhalese nationalism

In order to understand the present conflict it is important to appreciate the identification, which is made in the minds of many people in Sri Lanka, of Buddhism with Sinhalese nationalism.

The great majority of the Sinhalese population is Buddhist. A small minority is Christian. The Tamil population is predominantly Hindu, although again a percentage is composed of Christians. Some of the people of Sri Lanka are Muslims. The percentages which have been given to me are as follows: Buddhists 69.3%; Hindus 15.5%; Christians 7.5%, and Muslims 7.5%.

Many Buddhists believe that Sri Lanka was consecrated by the Buddha. The country is one of the major centres in the world for the Buddhist religion. It is claimed that the Buddhism which exists in Sri Lanka is the closest to the teachings of Buddha, to pure Buddhism. Buddhism has been preserved in Sri Lanka while, in surrounding regions, other religions have taken over. Many people virtually equate being Sinhalese and being Buddhist. Moves towards separatism are seen as a threat to both the Sinhalese race and to Buddhism.

Both succeeding governments and political parties in opposition have been guilty of appealing to these feelings solely to secure short-term political advantage. Whenever the government in power has been approaching agreement with Tamil leaders to remove some of the causes for Tamil grievance, the party out of power, whichever it has happened to be, has appealed to Sinhala-Buddhist nationalism. More than once the result has been to prevent implementation of any agreement reached. Members both of the UNP and SLFP, the two largest parties, and other parties and pressure groups, have used, and continue to use, these tactics.

As a result, Sinhala-Buddhist feelings, fanned as they have been for political gain, have given rise to militance, intolerance and acts of violence, all committed in the name of this peaceful religion. During the July 1983 disturbances, it seemed clear that the activities of some fervent followers of the Buddhist faith had been instrumental in stirring up anti-Tamil religious fervour, and had helped provide the background of tension against which the July violence took place. There were reports of the frequent repeating of chants expressing the sentiment that 'Sri Lanka is for the Sinhalese and for the Buddhists', in contra-distinction to the country being home to all Sri Lankans. Booklets have been distributed urging the Sinhalese to save Sri Lanka for Buddhism, and many people interviewed said that Buddhist monks and students from Buddhist schools had been amongst the mobs on the streets in July.

Recently an encouraging move has been made by some young Buddhist monks, who are trying to calm these heightened feelings and re-educate people to look again at the true teachings of Buddhism, to see for themselves that it does not advocate racism. This move is covered in more detail in the sub-section on initiatives to re-establish trust within the country, (IIIE). It is to be hoped that this view will prevail. At present, however, Sinhala-Buddhist sentiments are still being appealed to not only by politicians but also by prominent Buddhist leaders; and they cannot be ignored when considering the inflamed passions within sectors of Sri Lankan society today.

In this context it is possible to appreciate the feelings which must have been generated by the attack made, on May 14th, 1985, upon civilians in the ancient city of Anuradhapura.

Anuradhapura, unlike the other locations of violence and atrocities perpetrated since July, 1983, is not situated in the Tamil-speaking areas of the country. It is a Sinhalese city in a Sinhalese area. It is a holy city for Buddhists.

Reports are not consistent, and, at the time of writing, early June 1985, I am in no position to ascertain the exact truth. Most of the reports indicate that Tamil militants drove into the city in army uniform, and attacked and killed more than 150 civilians there. Hundreds more were wounded. Some of those killed were worshippers at Sri Maha Bodhi. This is the shrine of the oldest known Bo tree in the world. The tree is believed to have been grown here, over two thousand years ago, from a sapling of the tree under which the Buddha attained enlightenment. It has been venerated as a sacred tree for centuries.

To Sinhalese, an attack by Tamil militants in this location shows complete defiance of, and contempt for, Buddhism. It invited a backlash.

However, in contrast to the inability, or unwillingness, to maintain control which characterised the situation during the disturbances of July 1983, in May 1985, the government and the security forces contained the potential reaction, and order in the southern part of the island was maintained. Despite this control, inevitably resentments have been heightened.

x) The minority syndrome — as perceived by different groups within Sri Lankan society

Several communities within Sri Lanka are fearful due to their positions as minorities. The Tamils in Sri Lanka forming, as they do, only 18.2% of the total population of the country, are a minority.

However, only twenty-two miles away across the Palk Straits, are the nearest shores of the state of Tamil Nadu in southern India, where more than 50,000,000 Tamils reside.

The Sinhalese themselves number about 12,000,000. They feel very insecure because, despite being a 74% majority in Sri Lanka, they are only a small minority within the South Asia region. Many Sinhalese people hold very deeply felt fears that India will intervene in Sri Lanka, support the cause of the Tamil minority, and establish Tamil supremacy by force if necessary. The Sinhalese fear that, should this happen, they will be reduced to a level of second-class citizens or forced out of the country, with nowhere to go.

Other communities within Sri Lanka are also starting to exhibit signs of anxiety due to their position as minorities. Christians generally, and Sinhalese Christians in particular, are beginning to feel isolated, and fearful as a minority. Some Muslims fear that they too may be singled out for attack. Since my visit in February 1985, what have been described as "Muslim-Tamil disturbances" have erupted in the eastern region. During these members of both the Muslim and the Tamil communities were killed, injured and had their property destroyed. I have heard varying accounts of how and why these incidents occurred. One version is that the violence began when Tamils attacked and killed Muslim civilians, some at prayer in a mosque, the Muslims then retaliated and attacked Tamils in nearby regions. On the other hand, it is reported that the 5 Tamil militant groups have denied any attacks, instead, according to this latter version, police commandos and gangs brought in from other districts instigated the riots. I am not in a position to draw any conclusions as to the truth of what happened.

What is clear is that the fears of different groups, whether originally realistic and legitimate or not, serve to heighten the level of tension in the community and thus make outbursts more likely. There is today a dangerous and frightening spiral of fears, non-communication, resentments and over-reaction which more and more is erupting in alarming episodes of violence.

xi) Growing Tamil militancy and the demand for a separate state
These then are the major background factors against which the Tamil

people within Sri Lanka have become determined to change the present situation, and to secure what they see as their due measure of recognition within the country.

The approach adopted by the Tamil community in its endeavour to achieve these ends was, for the first thirty years after Independence, a peaceful one. As mentioned already, the Tamils sought a federal arrangement within one united country, not a separate state, and did not resort to, or advocate, violence as a means of achieving this. Indeed, their response to the attacks of violence against them which erupted in 1958, 1977, 1981 and 1983 has been very restrained. So also has been their response to the repeated disappointments, mentioned ealier, when concessions gained from negotiations with earlier governments failed to be given implementation.

In the mid 1970s, disillusioned with the results achieved so far, and feeling that they were steadily losing ground, the Tamil political parties re-formed themselves as one party, the TULF, (the Tamil United Liberation Front), which adopted separatism as one of its election platforms, although with the stated aim of achieving this through negotiation and not by force. On this platform the TULF gained all the seats in the northern part of the country, some of those in the eastern region, and became the major opposition party at the time of the last general election in 1977.

At about the same time a small group of Tamil youth declared its intention to establish a separate state and began to resort to violence. For the most part these acts of violence were not supported by the rest of the Tamil community, and they were not condoned by the Tamil Members of Parliament. Many Tamils, particularly those in the southern parts of the island, continued to be opposed to the idea of a separate state. The Tamil militants remained a very small group until very recently.

At first it appeared that their targets in the main were Tamil members of the police force, Tamil members and supporters of the ruling UNP party and moderate Tamil politicians who do not support separatism. The explanation is that these people are seen by the militants as co-operating with the government. However, more recently, they have attacked Sinhalese also and the 13 soldiers killed in the ambush on 23rd July 1983 were all Sinhalese.

The *Sri Lanka Newsletter* (a government publication) of September 20, 1983, p.11, states:

"The prime target of these terrorists were the Tamil politicians who held office in the Government or who supported the Government and the Police Force that was stationed in the North of Sri Lanka. The first victim was the Mayor of Jaffna, Mr. Alfred Duraiappa, who was assassinated in July 1975. The first police officer to be killed was Mr. Karunanidhi: in February 1977. To date 50 police officers and servicemen [this would include the 13 killed in the July 23 ambush], 11 politicians, 13 informants and 16 civilians have been killed, making a total of 90. Besides these killings, the terrorists have staged four major Bank robberies, attacked two police stations, destroyed an aircraft, set fire to public transport and government vehicles and sent parcels to prominent politicians and police officers."

To the militant groups' violent activities must be attributed in no small measure the inflammation of ethnic tensions which have so tragically erupted in violence. Sinhalese have reacted angrily to reports of Sinhalese military personnel being killed by the guerilla tactics of the terrorists. Also attacks on politicians and on policemen in the north have inflamed passions and done nothing to resolve the problems.

In addition, the determination of the militants to secure Eelam, a separate state for the Tamil people, is seen as a divisive move by Sinhalese people.

The numbers of the militants are variously estimated, but in the early years were not generally considered to be very high. Estimates I heard during my first visit in August 1983 ranged from as low as 60-100 to as high as 1500-2000. There are allegations that some of their number have been trained in places such as Libya, East Germany, with the IRA and the PLO, and more recently it was alleged they were being trained in Wales.

In the past couple of years, however, their numbers have risen and they are increasingly well armed and well trained. Despite denials from the Indian government, available evidence would seem to indicate that this has been achieved, in part, with assistance from the state of Tamil Nadu in southern India. As already indicated this connection with Tamil Nadu is of great concern to the Sinhalese.

It would appear that, in addition to any assistance received from Tamil Nadu, some funding is provided to the Tamil militants by ex-patriate Tamil groups located in different countries. Further, the militants to-day receive greater sympathy, and often support, from the Tamil population within Sri Lanka, particularly from those people residing in the north and east.

Recently the acts of violence perpetrated by the militants in their bid to secure a separate state by force have escalated sharply.

Tamil militants have attacked police stations and armed patrols, killing and maiming hundreds of members of the security forces; they have destroyed bridges, roads and railway tracks, blown up lorries, buses and trains; attacked both privately owned and state owned property, raided court houses, destroyed court records; attacked farming and fishing villages, in the very recent past they have, for the first time, attacked and killed unarmed Sinhalese civilians. They have also summarily executed people from their own community whom they suspect to be informers, or whom they deem to be anti-social in some way, i.e.

violating, for example by corruption, the standards which they feel should prevail in society.

As observed in the earlier LAWASIA report, violence, as a solution to problems, though the reasons behind the dissatisfaction may be understood, cannot be condoned. It is an infringement of the basic rights of those affected by it, increases the tension and distrust between communities, and makes an ultimate permanent solution very much more difficult. Until recently the conduct of most Tamil people in Sri Lanka would have indicated that they, too, opposed an approach of force.

Today, however, despite these repeated acts of violence, and despite the peaceful methods historically pursued by Tamil activists, more and more Tamil people have begun to regard the militants as their only hope of salvation from the actions of a government which they increasingly see as brutal, racist and repressive.

B. Some measures taken by the present government in its attempts to curb both Tamil militancy and the demand for a separate state

The measures which have been taken by the government in its attempts to check the rise of Tamil militancy and the demand for a separate state have, in many cases, unfortunately proved counter-productive. They have, instead of resolving the problem, fuelled the tensions, and driven the Tamil population more and more to a position from which they feel that they can co-exist with a Sinhalese-dominated government only if they have a separate state.

This is particularly unfortunate as the present government clearly recognised, in its 1977 election manifesto, the need to take positive action to ameliorate Tamil grievances, and has taken some steps with this aim in view. Also, since it came to power, the government has taken steps in the international arena which indicate a public commitment to human rights principles. (This aspect of government activity is covered in more detail later in the sub-section concerned with these initiatives, IIID).

i) The State of Emergency — background
It is important to consider the State of Emergency (proclaimed when violence erupted on the occasion of the May 18, 1983 municipal and Parliamentary by-elections, and in existence ever since) in the context of the general political situation within Sri Lanka. Accordingly a brief background follows. This background touches upon the 1977 election, the composition of Parliament, the promulgation of the 1978 Constitution, the Articles it contains regulating the duration of the office

of the President and the Parliament, the 1982 Presidential election and the 1982 referendum to extend the life of Parliament, and finally the municipal and Parliamentary by-elections held on May 18th 1983.

Since Independence the country has followed a system of multi-party parliamentary democracy. Two parties, the SLFP and the UNP, have alternated in power since 1948. Until now each general election has brought a sharp swing from one of these parties to the other.

The present government came into office on July 23rd, 1977. As a result of the 1977 general election, out of a total of 168 Parliamentary seats, the UNP (presently the ruling party) gained 140 seats. The TULF, a Tamil Party and the major opposition party, won 17 seats, and the remaining seats were divided between several parties, most of them being held by the SLFP, the party of which Mrs. Bandaranaike was formerly the leader.

The *1978 Constitution* contains the following provisions relevant to the present discussion: firstly, under it both the President and the Parliament hold office for a six year term (Articles 30 and 161), the President's term expiring in February 1984 (Articles 31 (4) and 160) and Parliament's term in August 1983, (Article 161 (e)); secondly, amendments to the *Constitution* require a two-thirds majority vote of all the members of Parliament, including those not present, (Article 82(5)). Since the ruling party holds such an overwhelming number of the Parliamentary seats it does not experience any problem in obtaining the requisite two-thirds majority.

In August 1982 the Third Amendment to the *1978 Constitution* was passed. This inserted a new provision, Article 31(3A), empowering the incumbent President to go to the people after only four of his six years in office, and to hold an election at that time seeking a mandate for a further term, instead of waiting until the expiration of the original six year period. The President chose to exercise this new power, and instead of waiting until February 1984, the Presidential election was held on October 20th 1982. President Jayewardene received 52.9% of the total number of votes polled and hence was elected for a new term in office. The Tamil minority opposed the election. In the Jaffna district only 46% of those eligible voted. In contrast, the national average of those who voted was 81% of those eligible.

Under the *Constitution* the next Parliamentary general election would normally have been held on the expiration of its six year term, in August 1983. Instead, however, a referendum was held in December 1982, two months after the Presidential election, to extend the life of the present Parliament by a further six year term. This by-passed the need for the August 1983 general election. Article 83 requires that for certain activities, including those "which would extend the term of office of the President and the duration of the Parliament, as the case may be, to over six years" two provisions must be satisfied. Firstly, two-thirds of the votes "of the whole number of Members (including those not present)" are required and secondly, approval "by the People at a Referendum" is necessary.

In accordance with this requirement a referendum was held. Of the votes cast, 54.6% were in favour of the extension of the term of office of the Parliament elected in 1977, from a six to a twelve year period. On this occasion the Tamil minority did vote. However, 95% of those voting in the Jaffna district voted 'No' to the extension of the life of Parliament, 5% voted 'Yes'. Of the 22 electoral districts, 15 voted in favour of the referendum, and 7 districts, including the districts with large Tamil populations, voted against the extension. (ICJ Update to the report by Virginia Leary).

Various allegations were made as to the unsatisfactory manner in which the referendum was conducted. Many people to whom I spoke had serious misgivings as to whether it had been carried out fairly. The Civil Rights Movement of Sri Lanka surveyed the events at the time and concluded that the manner of conducting the referendum may not have been "free and fair". Further, many people expressed the opinion that, had a general election been held, the UNP would no longer have retained the large number of seats which it had won in 1977.

On May 18th municipal elections were held, and, in addition to these local elections, by-elections were held in 18 constituencies in which the government party had failed to obtain a majority in the December referendum. This was done as a result of a decision made by the President. Of these 18 seats the UNP won 14. On this occasion there was considerable dissatisfaction with the procedures used, and many petitions contesting the validity of the results were lodged.

It was at the time of these elections that the violence occurred which prompted the government to proclaim a state of emergency.

ii) The state of emergency and the emergency regulations — their legality

In Sri Lanka, in addition to the requirement that states of emergency must be proclaimed, the occasion thereof must be communicated immediately to the Parliament (Article 155(4)). This was done. If Parliament is not in session it must be summoned to meet within ten days (Article 155(4)). The proclamation declaring the state of emergency (and bringing any emergency legislation into existence) will expire within fourteen days unless approved by a resolution of Parliament. A slightly longer period may operate where Parliament is not in session at the time and has to be summoned to meet (Article 155(6)). Subject to these requirements of Article 155(6), Article 155(5) povides that proclamations bringing the public security legislation into operation are valid for a period of one month, although a proclamation may be revoked at an earlier date.

The emergency regulations were brought into existence by proclamation. This is required by Article 155(3) of the *Constitution*. Such a procedure is in line with that contemplated by the *International Covenant on Civil and Political Rights* (Article 4(1)), and the procedure used was in accordance with the requirements of the Sri Lankan *Constitution*.

If emergency regulations continue in existence for a period of more than ninety consecutive days or a total period of ninety days during six consecutive calendar months, then, before the state of emergency can be continued for a further period of more than ten days within the next six calendar months, it must be approved by a resolution passed by at least two-thirds of the whole number of members of Parliament including those members not present (Article 155(8)). Again, a slightly longer period applies if Parliament is not sitting at the time. Without such a resolution the proclamation and the emergency legislation will lapse (Article 155(10)).

The authority for the making of the emergency regulations is as follows: under Section 5 of the *Public Security Ordinance*,

"the President may make such regulations...as appear to him to be necessary or expedient in the interests of public security and the preservation of public order and the suppression of mutiny, riot or civil commotion or for the maintenance of supplies and services essential to the life of the community."

Under Article 155(2)

"The power to make emergency regulations under the Public Security Ordinance ... shall include the power to make regulations having the legal effect of over-riding, amending or suspending the operations of the provisions of any law, except the provisions of the Constitution."

Emergency regulations lapse with the coming to an end of the proclamation of the state of emergency.

In summary, the emergency regulations, the proclamation bringing them into effect, and the existence of a state of emergency were in compliance with the terms of the Sri Lankan *Constitution* and of the *Public Security Ordinance*. It must be noted that the *Constitution* gives ultimate control over the duration of a state of emergency to the Parliament and does not leave it with the Executive. This is a most valuable safeguard. However, when the government possesses an overwhelming majority of the seats in Parliament such a situation minimises the effectiveness of this check.

iii) The emergency regulations which establish prohibited and security zones in the north and east

The emergency regulations considered in this sub-section were promulgated in late November 1984, and declare certain areas in the north to be "prohibited" zones and others to be "security" zones. These regulations, if strictly implemented, necessarily must cause massive disruption to the normal civilian life of the regions affected, and the reports I heard indicate that normal life has indeed ceased to exist.

Continuation with employment is said to have been made either extremely difficult or completely impossible. The regulations provide that no person may enter, or remain in, a prohibited zone for any purpose whatsoever without written authority. Some public buildings, e.g. hospitals and council offices, are in areas prohibited to access. The entire coastline from Mullaitivu to Mannar, (later extended from Kudremalai Point to Kokkilai), has been declared a prohibited zone to a distance of one hundred metres inland from the beach and extending five miles out to sea. Since a sizeable proportion of the population of the Jaffna district lives very close to the shore between Ponnalai and Point Pedro, full implementation of this regulation will force the dislocation of very many people. Already thousands of families are reported to have been evacuated from the prohibited zones to camps, and the fishing industry is at a standstill. More than 20,000 families of the fishermen, and others dependent upon the industry, are apparently left with no income.

The regulations do provide that any person who is deprived of his means of livelihood or his normal source of income as a result of these restrictions may seek relief from the Competent Authority. However, in many cases the severe curtailment of all movement, the location of relevant offices within the prohibited zones, and the general breakdown of services would seem to mean that it is difficult, if not impossible, for the affected persons to obtain such relief. Further, I was told that in some areas the relief offered was only Rs.1.75 per head per day; hardly, it was said, sufficient for a single meal.

Within the security zones there is strict curtailment of all movement. The regulations provide that no one may enter or leave such a zone without informing the Assistant Government Agent there. Permits are required for every vehicle — even for bicycles. The permit must be prominently displayed. Continued possession of the vehicle, without a permit, is an offence. Use of any such vehicle requires written authorisation also. Travel, when authorised, is restricted to certain hours and specific routes. Fuel is rationed. Private buses are not operating. State buses operate within strict limits.

Long curfews, up to sixty-one hours at a time, are reported to have been imposed. Schooling has been affected. In fact I was told that many schools cannot be used because dislocated people have taken refuge in school buildings. People often are unable to get to doctors or to hospitals for medical treatment. On occasions doctors themselves have been unable to get to the hospitals. I heard that all sorts of problems were arising. One mentioned to me was that people in the north are now dying of rabies, that they are unable to obtain the anti-rabies vaccine, both because of shortages in supply and because of the difficulties in getting to hospitals, and that rabid dogs are at large because the normal system under which these animals are kept under control has broken down.

Due to curfews and other restrictions farmers cannot tend or harvest their crops, or transport the crops to markets for sale, and farms are not being irrigated. Reports indicate that factories cannot operate without their supplies of materials and fuel, and workers often are unable to travel to work. The postal service is unreliable, much mail is not getting through, stamps are extremely difficult to obtain. Many people and their families are now without any incomes at all.

Criminal activity is increasing as law and order collapses. Civil administration is said to have broken down.

Further, the conditions of the people who have been moved to camps is reported to be very serious, with outbreaks of dysentery and diseases. Many essential sevices have ground to a halt, and there are reported to be grave shortages of food, fuel, medical and other supplies.

The result is deprivation, hardship and suffering to the people in these regions, and an exodus each day of great numbers of Tamils fleeing across the Palk Straits to southern India. In May, 1985, over 100,000 Tamils from northern Sri Lanka were said to be in camps in Tamil Nadu.

Sri Lanka is a signatory to *The International Covenant on Economic, Social and Cultural Rights*. Many of the rights protected by this Covenant cannot be enjoyed at the present time by those of her citizens who reside in the areas declared to be security and prohibited zones.

One of the effects of the emergency regulations, and their mode of implementation, has been a growing feeling amongst the Tamil people that the government has identified the entire Tamil population of the north and east, and not just the militant elements, as its enemy. There is consequently increasing fear and resentment of the government amongst the civilian population.

iv) Other emergency regulations

Many of the regulations adopted under the *Public Security Ordinance* concern supervision, search, arrest and detention (e.g. Regulations 16, 17, 18, 19, 20). These regulations are very wide in scope and are capable of being used to hold people in detention for long periods. They have been so used, and some of the people held under them have been held incommunicado without access to either lawyers or relatives. For instance, according to all the reports that I heard during my first visit in August 1983, the members of the leftist parties arrested at that time under the emergency regulations were at first held incommunicado, being denied both access to lawyers and visits by relatives. After an initial period, some, if not all of them, were permitted visits by some relatives. The denial of access to lawyers continued. Such detention amounts to a breach of Articles 9 and 14 of *The International Covenant on Civil and Political Rights*. These Articles preserve to individuals freedom from arbitrary arrest and detention, the right to be informed at the time of arrest of the reason for that arrest and of any charges, the right to be brought promptly before a justice, and to be tried within a reasonable time or released, the right to a fair trial, to be tried without undue delay, and the right to communicate with counsel of the detainee's own choosing.

Although a state of emergency has been proclaimed, some of the restrictions imposed by the regulations being here considered, and of those regulations establishing prohibited and security zones, have been imposed in a manner and in circumstances that go beyond the limits of measures strictly required by the exigencies of the situation.

Of the emergency regulations, Regulation 15A has called forth the most severe criticism of all. This regulation concerned the disposal of dead bodies. It removed a vital safeguard which serves to protect human life when it placed the decision as to the disposal of bodies, not with a member of the judiciary, but with a senior member of the police force and a member of the executive. Regulation 15A has been criticised by all international human rights organisations which have commented upon it. It was discussed at some length in the full version of my first report. Amnesty International condemned the regulation on the ground that it

"allows the police to bury or cremate the bodies of dead people if they deem it necessary — without anyone else being present and without inquest procedures ... a dangerous provision which could facilitate the deliberate extra-judicial executions of suspects in police and army custody". (*AI Newsletter*, July 1983).

The government has heeded such criticisms, and it is pleasing to note that Regulation 15A has now been repealed. However, another regulation, Regulation 55A-G, has been enacted in its stead. Regrettably, this regulation still does not confer the safeguards which exist under normal inquest procedures. By it the burial or cremation of dead bodies are still allowed at the order of the Deputy Inspector-General of Police. This official, it is true, is generally required by Regulation 55D(1) to hand bodies to the relatives of the deceased person, but, under Regulation 55D(2), he may instead order their cremation or burial "in the interest of national security or for the maintenance or preservation of public order in accordance with such steps as he may deem necessary in the circumstances".

Regulation 55A provides that any police officer or member of the armed forces causing the death of any person is to be detained in police or in military custody, and Regulation 55B provides that,

"Where a police officer or a member of the armed services has reason to believe that the death of any person may have been caused as a result of any action taken in the course of duty either by him or by any officer subordinate to him, or where any person dies in police custody or military custody..."

the facts relating to the death must be reported to the Inspector-General of Police, or to the nearest Deputy Inspector-General of Police.

Upon receipt of the information required by Regulation 55B the Inspector-General of Police, (or Deputy), must direct an officer not below the rank of Assistant Superintendent to proceed to the scene and make enquiries. Where the body is found, that fact must be reported to the magistrate. The magistrate, upon receiving a report from the Inspector-General, must then direct a Government Medical Officer to hold a *post mortem*, and then order that the body be handed over to the Deputy Inspector-General of Police for disposal.

The High Court in Colombo is given exclusive jurisdiction to enquire into the cause of death of any person occurring in the circumstances specified in Regulation 55B (Regulation 55E(1)), and shall hold an inquiry into such death whenever application is made to the court by the Inspector-General of Police. The enquiry may be held in any part of Sri Lanka. From the information available to me in February, 1985, it seemed that the enquiries are all held in Colombo, since the High Court judge is there.

The required procedure for these hearings is unsatisfactory as the High Court judge at no time sees the body. Further, I was told that the doctor does not appear in the court to give evidence. His medical report is simply forwarded to the High Court, as are the reports of the police upon the preliminary enquiries made by them. I was told, however, that the police sometimes do appear in court. The High Court proceedings are closed to the public. Although representatives of the deceased's family may be present, as far as I was able to ascertain no such representative has yet appeared. In light of this it appears unclear whether or not the notices which have been sent to the families of the deceased are reaching them. In any case it would be difficult, expensive and sometimes dangerous, for the family members to travel to Colombo for the hearings. There is no provision for lawyers to represent the deceased's family at the proceedings.

Regulation 55F gives a wide discretion to the Attorney-General. It provides that upon receiving the record of evidence, the Attorney-General may, if he is satisfied that the commission of any offence has been disclosed, direct the institution of proceedings under normal criminal law.

Regulation 55A-G is still no substitute for a normal inquest. This inquest is conducted in public. The deceased's family and the judicial officer have the opportunity to view the body, and discrepancies, if any, with the findings in the medical report can be observed. The doctor is present in court. The magistrate has the power to summon all the relevant witnesses. Lawyers are able to make submissions, and the public can see that the verdict is reached by an independent judicial officer and how this is done.

It is recommended that Regulation 55A-G be repealed, and that normal inquests be required to be held in all cases where persons have died after acts of violence. The existence of this procedure, in itself, would help prevent more indiscriminate killings. Further, by its introduction, the government could go some way towards restoring the confidence of Tamil people that there is no official condonation of killings of civilians by security forces; that, on the contrary, measures will be taken, and enforced, to ensure that these depradations cease.

v) Press coverage, propaganda and censorship regulations

Emergency regulations have been issued controlling meetings, organisations and publications. Some of the regulations in existence in July 1983 are considered here. They included: Regulation 12 controlling meetings and processions; Regulation 14 giving censorship powers; Regulation 28 regulating the distribution of leaflets; Regulation 30, regulating the printing or publishing of certain types of documents; and Regulation 68 controlling the proscribing of organisations. In combination these regulations make possible severe curtailment of the rights of freedom of speech and the expression of political opinion.

Curtailment of these freedoms is sometimes necessary to preserve order. However, it is desirable that no more restrictions are created than the exigencies of the situation really demand.

Under Regulation 68, the 3 leftist parties were proscribed on July 30th, (and, as is discussed elsewhere, other action taken included the arrest of some of their members). No information was given to the public which substantiated the allegations of the involvement of the parties in the violence, although this was the justification for the proscription (and for the arrests). This gives rise to serious concern for political freedom. No information substantiating these allegations had been given to the public when this delegation left Sri Lanka on September 1st, 1983, nor had it been provided by the time of the second LAWASIA mission, in February 1985.

Further, though less serious, the prohibition of the publication of papers and the sealing of presses would seem to be going further than was necessary since stringent censorship regulations did exist, and penalties had been introduced to control publications detrimental to national security. As has been noted already, the powers granted under this legislation were being thoroughly implemented by the government censor. Also, although there were no allegations of involvement by the SLFP in the July 1983 disturbances, nevertheless the paper of this party was banned and its presses sealed under authority given by the regulations.

Since that time, and indeed throughout the whole period of the state of emergency, despite frequently imposed, and sometimes extremely strict, censorship regulations there has been failure to control inflammatory propaganda calculated to provoke anti-Tamil sentiments. Such propaganda appears in the Sri Lankan press and even emanates from government sources. Furthermore, selective and partial reporting has resulted in misleading impressions being given. For instance, many attacks perpetrated by the armed forces on unarmed Tamil civilians are not given coverage in the press. This was the case, for example, when members of the security forces killed over 50 civilians in reprisal attacks carried out in the Jaffna area on July 24th, 1983. In contrast the ambush and killing of 13 Sinhalese soldiers by Tamil militants on the preceding day was given full coverage.

Although, until recently, there had been very few attacks made by Tamil militants on Sinhalese civilians, such attacks as are made receive extensive publicity. I have received, from several government sources, booklets containing colour photographs and graphic descriptions of the injuries said to have been incurred by Sinhalese victims in farming and fishing villages attacked by Tamil militants in late 1984. Similarly detailed coverage is not given to any of the many reprisal attacks on Tamil civilians by the security forces. For information about these attacks generally, resort must be had to the monitoring which is carried out by human rights bodies, and to the Tamil press which is based outside Sri Lanka.

Another disturbing factor is the existence of anti-Tamil propaganda booklets which have issued from government sources, notably under the aegis of Mr. Cyril Mathew. Mr. Mathew was the Minister of Industries and Scientific Affairs. In late December, 1984, Mr. Mathew was dismissed from the Cabinet by the President for "violations of the rules and conventions of cabinet government" after he had publicly criticised the draft legislation put forward at the end of the All Party Conference meetings.

Propaganda issued under a Minister's auspices necessarily appears to have the imprimatur of the government.

On the other hand, anti-Sinhala and sometimes vitriolic press has been produced from some Tamil sources outside Sri Lanka, and this also has exacerbated the situation, although its effect within the country is presumably a great deal less than that of publications which are freely available there, and those issuing from official origins. On either side any such material can do nothing but increase the problems.

It is in the long-term interests of all Sri Lankan people that a policy of balanced and comprehensive reporting be pursued in all news coverage. The government, because it is the government, is in a position to exercise both control and leadership in this regard. If this is not done resentments and misunderstandings will continue to be fanned by the propagation of biased, inaccurate, misleading or incomplete reports.

At the time of my second enquiry, censorship restrictions were still in force in the country. All news and pictorial reports relating to terrorism, terrorist activity, similar acts of violence, security operations of the armed services and police, and news relating to the unrest then affecting universities were to be submitted to the Competent Authority prior to publication. I was told that all newspapers were submitted to the censor daily before their publication.

vi) The Prevention of Terrorism Act

This legislation was enacted in 1979 as a temporary measure and entitled *The Prevention of Terrorism (Temporary Provisions) Act*. In July 1982 the Act, despite the indications of its temporary nature still contained in its title, was made a part of the permanent law of the land. This step gives cause for considerable concern as the legislation (hereinafter, for the sake of brevity, referred to as *The Prevention of Terrorism Act*), contains provisions which are in conflict with several of the articles of *The International Covenant on Civil and Political Rights* to which Sri Lanka is a signatory.

Any government undeniably has an extremely difficult task when dealing with intransigent militant groups bent on achieving their aims through violent methods. However, removal of the causes, the grievances which are seen to provide a rationale for the violence, is the only effective way to resolve the problem in the long term. Further, on the practical side, there is a good deal of evidence, both from experience within Sri Lanka and elsewhere, which suggests that harsh legislation of this kind does not in fact assist in combatting insurgency.

In Sri Lanka it seems clear that support for the militant groups has grown in the northern and eastern provinces as more and more has been heard about the ill-treatment of those held in detention under the authority of *The Prevention of Terrorism Act*.

Under the legislation those "connected with or concerned in or reasonably suspected of being connected with or concerned in any unlawful activity" become, without any further justification, subject to the exercise of very wide powers. "Unlawful activity" is a concept which receives an extremely wide definition and embraces comparatively minor offences. (See Articles 2 and 31).

The powers conferred by this legislation have been used almost exclusively against Tamils. They permit arrests, without warrant, of *Prevention of Terrorism Act* suspects, search of premises and vehicles, seizure of documents, the taking of persons "to any place" for interrogation, the taking of measures for identification, and the restriction of these persons' movements and activities. (Sections 6,7,11). The Act brings within its ambit even actions committed *before* its enactment, although at the time that the acts were committed they may not have contravened any law then in existence (Section 31).This brings Sri Lanka into contravention with Article 15(1) of *The International Covenant on Civil and Political Rights* which provides,

"No one shall be held guilty of any criminal offence on account of any act or omission which did not constitute a criminal offence, under national or international law, at the time when it was committed."

Section 9 provides that suspects under the Act may be detained "in such place and subject to such conditions as may be determined by the Minister", and that detainees may be held without trial for successive periods of three months up to a maximum of eighteen months. Detainees are often held not in ordinary prisons, but in army camps, and sometimes in police stations. Even when charged and awaiting trial, and during trial, the Secretary to the Minister may order the detainee to be held in any place and subject to any conditions he directs (Section 15A).

The Act provides for prison terms which range from five to twenty years, and life imprisonment, for accused persons who are convicted. There is no requirement that detainees be brought before a magistrate upon detention. Section 13 does provide that detainees may make representations, in respect of the detention or restriction orders concerning them, to an Advisory Board of 3 persons appointed by the President. The orders of this Board are "final and shall not be called in question in any court by way of writ or otherwise" (Section 10). Dr. Ranjit Amerasinghe, Secretary, Ministry of Justice, who is one of the members of the Advisory Board, told me that detainees, or their families, regularly apply to the Board and use this procedure as a means of expediting consideration of their cases. He told me that there had been 225 applications to the Board between August, 1984 and mid-February, 1985.

In some instances the person has been released by the time the Board hears the case. In the instances where there appears to be a *prima facie* case against the detainee, Dr. Amerasinghe said that a request is made by the Board for expedition of the proceedings. In other cases release is recommended, sometimes subject to Section 11. Section 11 provides that suspects under the Act may be subjected to orders restricting their movements, and/or their activities with associations or organisations and political activities.

Other provisions of *The Prevention of Terrorism Act* remove some of the protections for accused persons which exist under the ordinary criminal law. The *Evidence Ordinance* provides that, unless made in the presence of a magistrate, no confession made in police custody is admissible in evidence. Under *The Prevention of Terrorism Act*, on the other hand, confessions made while the detainee is in police custody are admissible in evidence, provided that they were not made to a police officer below the rank of Assistant Superintendent, unless the detainee is able to prove that the statements are "irrelevant". They are "irrelevant" for instance, if obtained under duress (Section 16). It would not be easy for a detainee to prove such an allegation. Other provisions, taking away the ordinary protections of the criminal law, are contained in Section 18 which concerns the admissibility of certain types of documents as evidence, and the procedure which may be adopted concerning contradictory statements of witnesses.

Finally, Section 26 provides,

"No suit, prosecution or other proceeding, civil or criminal, shall lie against any officer or person for any act or thing in good faith done or purported to be done in pursuance or supposed pursuance of any order made or direction given under this Act."

There has been sustained criticism of the harshness of the provisions of *The Prevention of Terrorism Act*, and the harshness of the implementation measures adopted, both from bodies within Sri Lanka and from international and regional human rights bodies outside the country.

Wide powers of detention without provisions for regular judicial review or for access by lawyers, relatives or friends invite abuse. When they are coupled with the holding of detainees in places other than the regular civilian prisons, which in Sri Lanka are administered subject to laws providing strict regulations for the welfare and protection of the prisoners, by their very nature they make possible, or even likely, the maltreatment of the detainees.

Detainees often have been held in army camps, incommunicado, without access to lawyers and relatives, and in some cases have been tortured and even killed while held in custody. Amnesty International has documented, and reported upon, a large number of allegations of assault and torture, and has concluded that political suspects held under The Prevention of Terrorism Act have been "frequently held incommunicado, sometimes for more than eight months, and that they had been tortured, both in army camps and by the police." (*AI Annual Report 1984*, p.258). In June, 1983 Mr. Tim Moore, MLA, of the Australian section of the ICJ, carried out enquiries into allegations of the torture of persons held in detention. He interviewed both former detainees and their families, and was convinced of the truth of many of the allegations.

In February, 1985, two Members of Parliament from the United Kingdom Parliamentary Human Rights Group, Robert Kilroy-Silk and Roger Sims, visited Boosa camp in southern Sri Lanka. At the time the camp contained 351 persons who had been detained under *The Prevention of Terrorism Act*. In their report it is stated,

"....it was clear to us all that the prisoners were cowed and afraid. It was also clear that very many — if not all of them — had been ill-treated. The torture — which seemed to take the form of beating, mainly on the buttocks with plastic pipes (we saw the terrible scars that such a beating leaves), being hung by the feet over a chilli fire, having pins pushed down finger nails, and lighted cigarettes snubbed out on the body — appears to be mainly carried out by the police at the point of arrest."

The kinds of ill-treatment documented above correspond to the descriptions given by other human rights organisations.

A few charges of ill-treatment have been heard by the courts in Sri Lanka. In 1981 the Court of Appeal found the allegations of assault made by 3 of the 4 detainees appearing before it to be established by the evidence. Relatives of the detainees had filed petitions for writs of *habeas corpus* under Article 141 of the *Constitution*. (Application Nos. 10/81, 11/81 and 13/81).

In another case it was found, at a *post mortem* examination, that the deceased detainee had suffered 25 external and 10 internal injuries which had been inflicted upon him by force. This was the case of Mr. A.K. Navaratnarajah who died on 10th April, 1983, whilst held in custody at the Gurunagar Army Camp. At the time of my visit in February, 1985, no-one had been charged with Mr. Navaratnarajah's murder.

Towards the end of 1984 there were reports from reliable sources that detainees held in camps in the north have been killed. Some of these killings are said to have occurred while the detainees were trying to escape. This was said to be the reason why approximately 22 detainees were killed at the army camp at Vavuniya.

All governments have the responsibility for the safe-keeping of those in their custody. It is urged that immediate, public and impartial investigations be instituted into the killings of the alleged escapees, and into all those cases in which detainees have been killed, or concerning whom allegations of torture or ill-treatment are made. It is important that those persons who were responsible for the deaths, and ill-treatment, be brought to trial in the ordinary criminal courts.

Failure to carry out such investigations and punishments will encourage the repetition of similar incidents. Government explanations that it is impossible to find reliable evidence to identify those responsible for such killings cannot be accepted in the absence of a clear indication of a serious, public and impartial attempt to investigate such events. Enquiries by the senior officers of those responsible is an inadequate response to actions as serious as these. It is urged that judicial enquiries be held into every death which occurs in custody.

It is hardly necessary to specify that killings and ill-treatment of detainees amount to a contravention of several of the provisions of the *International Covenant on Civil and Political Rights* to which Sri Lanka is a signatory. The rights infringed are:- the right to life (Article 6), the right to be not subjected to torture or cruel, inhuman or degrading treatment or punishment (Article 7), and Article 10, "All persons deprived of their liberty shall be treated with humanity and with respect for the inherent dignity of the human person."

In relation to other aspects of the legislation and its implementation Article 9(3) of the *International Covenant* provides that,

"Anyone arrested or detained on a criminal charge shall be brought promptly before a judge or other officer authorised by law to exercise judicial power and shall be entitled to trial within a reasonable time or release."

Provisions of *The Prevention of Terrorism Act* and the ways in which they have been applied do not conform with this requirement, nor do they comply with Article 9(2) which states,

"Anyone who is arrested shall be informed, at the time of arrest, of the reasons for his arrest and shall be promptly informed of any charges against him."

I was told, by reliable sources, that this provision is very often not observed.

Article 14 is also contravened. This Article requires *inter alia* that persons should be tried without undue delay, and be allowed to communicate with counsel of their own choosing.

The conflict with the provisions of Article 15 (retrospective creation of criminal offences) has been mentioned already .

The government points to the fact that the legislation is directed against terrorism, that the country is in a declared state of emergency, and that Article 4 of *The International Covenant on Civil and Political Rights* does permit derogations from some of its provisions.

Article 4(1) provides that,

"In time of public emergency which threatens the life of the nation and the existence of which is officially proclaimed, the States Parties to the present Covenant may take measures derogating from their obligations under the present Covenant to the extent strictly required by the exigencies of the situation, provided that such measures are not inconsistent with their other obligations under international law and do not involve discrimination solely on the ground of race, colour, sex, language, religion or social origin."

As can be seen, in order for derogations to be permissible under Article 4, there must be a "public emergency which threatens the life of the nation", the existence of that public emergency must be "officially proclaimed" and the measures taken must not exceed "the extent strictly required by the exigencies of the situation."

As mentioned already a state of emergency has been continuously in force in Sri Lanka since May 18, 1983. Prior to that date states of emergency had been declared by the present government for several brief periods. It should be noted that, so far, this government has made less extensive use of declarations of states of emergency than did its predecessor, which ruled for almost six years under a state of emergency.

Whether there is in fact presently a "public emergency threatening the life of the nation" depends, of course, upon the exact meaning of this expression. An identical phrase appears in the *European Convention on Human Rights*, and the European Court, in the *Lawless Case* (1 EHRR 15) interpreted the phrase as follows,

"an exceptional situation of crisis or emergency which affects the whole population and constitutes a threat to the organised life of the community of which the State is composed."

It is possible for such a situation to exist in a part or parts of a country only. This may well be the situation in Sri Lanka at the present time. Certainly, prior to the recent escalation of violence, except for brief periods such as the time of the disturbances in July 1983, it could be doubted whether the declaration of a state of emergency covering the entire island was in fact justified by the circumstances. Now, at least in the north and east, it is more likely that more people would consider that the situation amounts to one of real emergency threatening the life of the nation. Ironically that situation may have been brought about, at least in part, by the very legislative provisions now in question and which are sought to be justified by the very tensions, and hence the emergency, which they have helped to generate.

In order to comply with the requirements of the International Covenant the emergency measures taken must be in proportion to the actual requirements. Until recently, the number of suspected militants and their activities were sufficiently small that *The Prevention of Terrorism Act* must have been viewed, in the circumstances then prevailing, as going beyond the measures "strictly required by the exigencies of the situation." Today, in the north and east the problem is more severe. Again, however, this would seem to be due, at least in part, to these very provisions, and their mode of implementation.

In any case *The Prevention of Terrorism Act* forms part of the permanent legislation of Sri Lanka, and has been in operation even when no state of emergency has been proclaimed. At such times the legislation clearly contravenes many of the articles of *The International Covenant on Civil and Political Rights*.

Even when a state of emergency is justified and is officially proclaimed, no derogation is allowed from three of the articles contravened, i.e. Articles 6, 7 and 15, right to life, freedom from torture or cruel, inhuman or degrading punishment, and retrospective creation of criminal offences. From the other articles derogation is allowed only "to the extent strictly required by the exigencies of the situation." Hence, even allowing for a "public emergency threatening the life of the nation", Sri Lanka is still in breach of some of her obligations under the Covenant.

Repeal of *The Prevention of Terrorism Act* would remove these contraventions of international norms. It would also have the beneficial effect of removing one of the current causes of the alienation of the Tamil people from the government. It is recommended that the legislation be repealed. Failing this, it is urged that at least those provisions and the forms of implementation which do bring Sri Lanka into conflict with her obligations under international law be immediately reconsidered, and the provisions be repealed or significantly amended.

vii) Mass arrests of young Tamil males

Reliable reports indicate that mass arrests have been made in some areas in the north of all the young Tamil males found there. The arrests are usually of those aged between 15 and 30, and are made on the ground that the race, age and sex of these young men makes it likely that they may be offenders. Many, but not all, are released after questioning but release can take a considerable time. Many of these people are transported to interrogation camps in the south where some have been held for several months. The families of these young men often do not learn of their whereabouts for a considerable period.

Arrests are made particularly after attacks by Tamil militant groups on security personnel. For example, according to a report published in the 18th December 1984 edition of *The Daily Telegraph*, London, the Sri Lankan government stated that 725 "terrorist suspects" were detained during the first week of December, 1984. The figures given by the Secretary of the Jaffna Citizens Committee, included in the same newspaper report, were to the effect that at least 1200 people had been arrested since November, 1984. Most of the detainees were said to be men between 18 and 30 years of age.

Many young men were reported to have been arrested on 4 August 1984, in Valvettithurai and Point Pedro after an attack on naval personnel made that day near to Point Pedro. On the 27 August 1984, the Minister for National Security, Mr. Lalith Athulathmudali is reported in *The Sun* newspaper, to have stated,

"There could well be innocent people among those taken into custody in connection with the Point Pedro and Valvettithurai incidents. But the true culprits can only be identified after an enquiry."

Over 500 persons were reported to have been transported from Valvettithurai and Point Pedro on August 4th, to Boosa Camp in the south of the island. Reliable reports indicate that many of them were held for several weeks, and some for several months before they were released. As noted earlier, at least some of these persons are reported to have been ill-treated while held in detention.

These methods of detention and interrogation have been justified by the government as necessary since Tamil civilians refuse to give to the authorities information about the militants. It is said that the civilians are making necessary the taking of such measures by their non-co-operation.

Although it is accepted that the government needs to take measures to control those who resort to violent activities, it is not open to a state which has acceded to *The International Covenant on Civil and Political Rights* to resort to measures of mass arrests, and sometimes lengthy detention, of persons who are neither a threat to national security nor suspected of having committed an offence. Arrests should be discriminating. They should be kept strictly within the confines of the exigencies of the situation. Enquiries should be expedited, and prompt release made of those against whom there is no evidence.

Furthermore, activities such as these are counter-productive. They must result in alienating both the young people in question and their families and friends from the present regime, and to this extent must be compounding the current problems.

viii) The passage of the Sixth Amendment

A constitutional amendment, the Sixth, now Article 157A(1) and (2), was enacted in August 1983. The Sixth Amendmement requires an oath to be taken in the following terms:

"I,......., do solemnly declare and affirm/swear that I will uphold and defend the Constitution...and that I will not, directly or indirectly, in or outside Sri Lanka, support, espouse, promote, finance, encourage or advocate the establishment of a separate state within the territory of Sri Lanka."

The effects of this Amendment were summarised by the Prime Minister at the second reading of the bill on August 4th as follows (Hansard pp. 1278, 1279):

"Then, what is the purpose of the sixth Amendment. The purpose is to provide the severest punishment to those who advocate or attempt to establish a separate State.

On whom do we impose these punishments?

We provide in paragraph (1) of the new Article 157 that 'No person shall, directly or indirectly, in or outside Sri Lanka, support, espouse, promote, finance, encourage or advocate the establisnment of a separate State within the territory of Sri Lanka.' In paragraph (2) we are prohibiting political parties, associations or organisations from having as their object the establishment of a separate State within Sri Lanka.

Accordingly, it would be seen that any person who even remotely supports the idea of a separate State commits an offence.

We have formulated the offence in the widest possible terms. As such no support can be given for separatism directly or indirectly or even from outside Sri Lanka.

The prohibition would apply not only to Sri Lankans but even to non-Sri Lankans whether they support terrorism inside or outside Sri Lanka.

A person who is guilty of such an offence would firstly be subject to the civic disabilities already prescribed under the Constitution.

Secondly, he would forfeit all his property both movable and immovable, as is determined by the Courts.

Thirdly, he would lose his rights to obtain a passport, to sit for any public examination, to own any immovable property even in the future and engage in any trade or profession for which he needs a licence or similar authorisation.

Finally, such a person would lose any public office he holds whether as a Member of Parliament or in the public service or in any State Corporation. It would therefore be seen that such a person would be legally incapacitated to the most drastic degree.

Political parties, associations and organisations which espouse separatism would become liable to be proscribed after judicial determination and any person who remains a member of such a party, association or organisation would suffer the same consequences that I just mentioned.

The power to convict a person for any offence relating to separatism will be granted to the Court of Appeal and the sentence would become effective despite any appeal to the Supreme Court.

In addition to the penal sanctions I have mentioned we are providing in Paragraph (7) of the new Article that all Members of Parliament, public officers, judicial officers and officers of public corporations and local authorities should take an oath or affirmation renouncing separatism. [All lawyers must take the oath renouncing separatism.]

We are also making such an oath or affirmation a pre-requisite for nomination as a Member of Parliament. This oath or affirmation has to be taken by such persons in addition to the oath or affirmation already taken under the Constitution. In Paragraph (8) of the new Article, power is given to Parliament to determine which other categories of persons or officers should take such an oath or affirmation.

The failure to take the oath or affirmation would immediately result in the loss of office."

One TULF MP told me that on the introduction of the Amendment into Parliament, his party sent a telegram to the Chief Justice stating its wish to challenge the Amendment's constitutionality in the Supreme Court, pointing out that, because of the violence and its effects on the general climate, there could be no rational discussion of the Amendment's legal and political ramifications at this time. The party also protested to the Chief Justice and to the government about the holding of the Sixth Amendment debate in Parliament in these circumstances, and requested a postponement. The debate was not postponed. The debate, the first, the second and third readings were all completed in one day. In the event a challenge to the Sixth Amendment was mounted in the Supreme Court, although not by the TULF.

Under Articles 120 and 121 of the *1978 Constitution* it is possible to challenge proposed legislation on the ground that it is inconsistent with

Changing Dangers: not time very th space

One safe be now at risk. Plates their were as well as time so that places their were coastal areas may experince more flooding in the future as a result of global warming.

Eg low-lying

e.g flooding may explain greater magnitude of flooding due to deforestation changing + i.e These examples show how humans can change location.

=>
HAZARD PERCEPTION + understanding
=> cost of living in area may cushion risk i.e
when e.g cultures say high risk of eruption by

RISK – people expose themselves to hazard.

People may consciously place themselves at risk
from natural hazards – why?

→ unpredictability – hazards are not always predictable.
may be difficult to know when a
where a event may occur or magnitude.

→ Lack of Alternatives – People stay in hazardous areas to
es ner active fault line at risk from earthquakes, may
Coyne → due to economic "tics" – or shortage of land.
+ knowledge –

the *Constitution*. Such a challenge must be mounted while the legislation is in the form of a bill. Once it has been enacted by the Parliament no further challenge is possible. If the Bill is described in its long title as being for the amendment of any provision of the *Constitution*, and the Sixth Amendment was so described, then Article 120(a) provides that,

"the only question which the Supreme Court may determine is whether such Bill requires approval by the People at a Referendum by virtue of the provisions of Article 83."

Article 83 provides *inter alia*, that bills to amend or repeal or replace any of the provisions of Articles 1,2,3,6,7,8,9,10,11 or 83 need a vote of two-thirds of the members (including those not present), approval by the people at a referendum, and a certificate endorsed thereon by the President.

Ordinarily the Supreme Court, which is the Court with the jurisdiction to hear the challenge, has a period of three weeks in which to make its decision (Article 121). However, the Court may be required to hand down its decision within a shorter time period (Article 122). The constitutional validity of the Sixth Amendment was challenged, and on this occasion the Court was required to give its opinion within twenty-four hours.

The finding of the Supreme Court was that the Sixth Amendment was in compliance with the *Constitution* except for two provisions relating to penalties (Hansard, August 4th, pp.1255, 1256). The Supreme Court held that these two provisions, as they stood, were inconsistent with Article 11, and therefore required, as well as passage by a two-thirds majority in Parliament, approval by the people at a referendum. Article 123(4) provides that :

"Where any Bill, or any provision of any Bill, has been determined ... to be inconsistent with the Constitution, such Bill or provisions shall not be passed except in the manner stated in the determination of the Supreme Court."

The government gave an undertaking to alter these two provisions so that the Amendment would be no longer inconsistent with Article 11. On that basis the Amendment was put before the Parliament on August 4th and, after a debate which ended in the early hours of August 5th, it was passed by the required two-thirds majority. The TULF boycotted this debate. The other parties supported the Amendment. As noted earlier, since one of the platforms of the TULF party consisted of support, through non-violent means, for a separate state, TULF MPs felt that to take the required oath would be a denial of the platform upon which they had been elected. As a result they forfeited their right to retain their parliamentary seats.

The political wisdom of the passage of the Sixth Amendment was queried immediately. Mr.A.Bandaranaike (member of the SLFP) had this to say in Parliament on August 4th,1983,

"Take the Tamil United Liberation Front for example. I hope they swear in on the 9th with the rest of us. But if they decide not to for some reason or the other, then the entirety of the North, 10 per cent of our population, will be unrepresented in this House for the first time since adult franchise since 1934; for the first time the Northern Tamil community of this country will be unrepresented in the legislature. I am not arguing the merits of their keeping out. I am not saying it is good or bad, but if for some reason of their own if they decide to keep out, you remove from the body politic the most important minority of this country, you remove them from the body politic. And what do you do with them thereafter or what will they do themselves? They will become prisoners in the hands of the terrorists and extremists in the North. Well, I concede the fact that terrorism and the 'tigers' were nurtured by the TULF. There is no doubt about that. But there are moderates in that party...But, Sir, if you remove this volatile minority from this House and you put them into the hands of the terrorists the extremists, let us consider I am not making any political declarations here in the House — the consequences of that Act..."

He was followed by Mr A. Moonesinghe (SLFP) who said,

"The situation is not as simple as the government portrays it to be. You may be able to tell the TULF to give up their demand for a separate state of Eelam and to come and sit here but they will find it very difficult to do that unless you are able, at the same time, to show them a way out of this situation. I feel that as far as this Amendment is concerned, you are not leaving room for the TULF to manoeuvre. You are going to deprive them of the right to own property, of the right to have resort to trade or to practise their profession. What are you really trying to do? We must leave them room to manoeuvre, to develop into a democratic opposition, a democratic system and for a democratic party to emerge in the North.

You can bring in all the laws and you have all the powers to do that but you do not have the power to win over the Tamil community. You must leave an avenue open for the democratic element in the North to come up. They have to give up their cry for Eelam -(Interruption). I do not think the Hon. Minister understood the point I was trying to make. The TULF themselves became victims of the political realities of the North."

The result of the Sixth Amendment has been that, since September 1983, at a time when they are particularly in need of an organised political group able to act on their behalf through the normal parliamentary process, and when it is particularly important to encourage Tamil participation in Sri Lankan political life, the Tamil people of the north, and some of the people of the east, find themselves in a situation in which they are no longer represented in Parliament. Their elected representatives, and the major opposition party, are no longer able to participate in the affairs of government.

(ix) The All Party Conference

An All Party Conference, a forum to discuss solutions to Tamil grievances, was promised by the present government in its 1977 election manifesto. The manifesto, in reference to these grievances stated, "such problems should be resolved, without loss of time". Such a conference, as part of the endeavour to resolve communal tensions and ease Tamil grievances, would have seemed to be a most desirable way of establishing dialogue between the different parties, thus making an effective solution much more likely. Unfortunately, although the government did engage in a dialogue with the TULF for a considerable period, six years went by before a conference of the type envisaged was called — in mid-July 1983, and then its terms of reference were limited to terrorism. As a result, many of the invited participants, including both the SLFP and the TULF parties, refused to attend.

After this first meeting of the Conference, in mid-July 1983, a second meeting was scheduled for the last week in July, 1983. In response to representations, the President had agreed that a much wider range of topics be discussed at this meeting. Unfortunately, the outbreak of disturbances prevented the holding of the second session of the Conference. The potential it may have had for a resolution of the ethnic problems and tensions within the country was not realised in time to prevent the eruption of violence.

After many delays the Conference was eventually convened on January 10th, 1984. Nine political parties were invited to participate in the proposed Conference meetings. These parties were:- the All Ceylon Tamil Congress, the Ceylon Workers' Congress (CWC), the Communist Party for Sri Lanka, the Democratic Workers' Congress (DWC), the Lanka Sama Samaja Party (LSSP), the Mahajana Eksath Peramuna (MEP), the Sri Lanka Freedom Party (SLFP), the Tamil United Liberation Front (TULF), and the UNP (United National Party), together with a delegation of government ministers. During the early meetings of the Conference it was decided to enlarge the participation and to invite representative bodies and associations other than political parties. As a result of this decision the following organisations were invited to participate in the deliberations: the Supreme Council of the Maha Sangha, the Christian organisations, the Sri Lanka Buddhist Congress, the Sinhala Associations, the Hindu Organisations, the All Ceylon Muslim League and the Council of Muslims of Sri Lanka.

Early in the proceedings two of the political parties, the SLFP and the MEP, withdrew from the deliberations.

The meetings of The All Party Conference were held throughout 1984. During this time there was discussion of various proposals which were put forward for an acceptable scheme of regional autonomy. One proposal, Annexure 'C', had been drawn up towards the end of 1983, consequent upon discussions which had been held in Colombo and New

Delhi. It had been agreed as the basis for discussion at the All Party Conference.

Proposals contained within the Annexure include the possibility of an amalgamation of district development councils within a province into regional councils. Regional councils were to have legislative and executive powers over specified subject areas. Details of this proposal were to be worked out later but, as a general policy, the powers of the regional councils were to include the maintenance of internal law and order in the region, the administration of justice, social and economic development, cultural matters and land policy. The regional councils were to be empowered also to levy taxes and mobilise resources through loans. In addition to this means of funding they were to receive allocations of funds from the central government. Provision was to be made for constituting High Courts in each region. The Supreme Court of Sri Lanka would exercise appellate and constitutional jurisdiction.

In Annexure 'C' it was proposed that the membership of the armed forces should reflect the national ethnic composition of the population. At the present time Sinhalese form a much higher proportion of the armed forces than their 74% of the total population, and it has been suggested that one way to reduce the tensions between the civilian population of the north and east and the members of the armed forces, would be to post Tamil personnel to those regions. It was further proposed that the police forces stationed in the north and east should reflect the ethnic compositon of those areas. This has already been tried to some extent in Jaffna. The proportion of Tamil policemen in Jaffna was greatly increased a few years ago, and relations between the civilian population and the police force were reported at the time to have improved a great deal.

In the Annexure it was proposed that Trincomalee port and harbour should be administered by a port authority which would be controlled by the central government.

It was agreed that a national policy on land settlement, and the basis on which the government is to undertake land colonisation in the future, would have to be worked out. The proposal was that settlement schemes should be based on ethnic proportions so as not to alter the demographic balance. Agreement was to be reached upon settlement schemes for major projects.

It was agreed that the present laws concerning the Sinhala and Tamil languages were to be accepted and implemented.

Despite general agreement at the outset upon these important basic premises, the All Party Conference collapsed in acrimony, without any agreement having been reached, in December 1984.

On December 14th, before this happened, the President set forth specific proposals in the form of draft legislation: the Tenth Amendment, the *District and Provincial Councils Bill*, and the *Local*

Authorities Bill — which together contained a proposal for local authorities, and further tiers of District and Provincial Councils. The Tenth Amendment contained also a proposal for the establishment of a second chamber of Parliament, to be called the Council of State, with 75 members to be appointed mainly from the District Councils.

In putting the draft legislation before the All Party Conference, and commending it to the careful consideration of all the delegates, the President described it as representing the considered views emerging from the negotiations. On December 21st, President Jayewardene told the All Party Conference Plenary Sessions that the leaders of all the delegations which had attended the sessions had agreed to his decision to put forward the legislation, saying that no objection to this step had been made by any delegate.

The President's position on subsequent events is outlined in the following terms in the address which he made to Parliament on February 20th, 1985,

"I was therefore surprised to read a statement by Mr. A. Amirthalingham, Leader of the TULF, in the 'Weekend' of Sunday 23rd December and in the *Ceylon Daily News* of Monday 24th December that the proposals are totally unacceptable to the Tamil people.

At its meeting on Wednesday 26th December 1984, the Cabinet therefore decided that, as the TULF has said that there was no purpose in discussing these proposals further, nothing could be achieved in discussing or arriving at a decision on them and therefore the Government will not implement these proposals".

In conversations I had with Mr. A. Amirthalingam when he visited Sydney in May 1985, he told me that the TULF had been consistent in its position throughout the negotiations that proposals such as those put forward by the President in mid-December would not be acceptable. He said the statement to the effect that the TULF had accepted, and then suddenly rejected, these proposals was incorrect.

On Sunday, December 23rd, *The Island* reported,

"Mr. Cyril Mathew, Minister of Industries and Scientific Affairs and a UNP stalwart, the Tamil United Liberation Front, and the SLFP leader Mrs. Sirima Bandaranaike yesterday issued statements rejecting the proposals put forward by the government for a solution to the communal problem following the Round Table Conference.

Mr. Mathew questioned the introduction of the Second Chamber, the position of Buddhism under the proposed amendments, the powers vested in District Councils and the official language used in District Councils under the proposed legislation.

Mrs. Bandaranaike said the legislation would not be a basis for a political solution, while the TULF said the proposed legislation would not result in autonomy or a genuine devolution of power ...

Mr. Mathew said ... he was 'unable to advise anyone to agree with the proposed legislation' on the ethnic problem ..."

The Daily News, of Sunday, December 24th, reported,

"In a statement he issued before leaving for Madras with other leaders of the Front, Mr. Amirthalingam states, '...We are constrained to state that the two bills before this conference do not embody any scheme of autonomy which could be accepted by the Tamil people or their accredited representatives, the Tamil United Liberation Front.'"

Later, the LSSP, (Lanka Sama Samaja Party), the Communist party and the SLMP (Sri Lanka Mahajana Party), were reported in *The Island*, February 10th, as saying,

"... the UNP government has not shown any serious desire to find a just and democratic settlement of estranged and embittered ethnic relations through political dialogue. Instead, it has followed policies that have made matters much worse and strengthened racist, divisive and separatist tendencies.

It dragged on the Round Table Conference for nearly a year and terminated it abruptly after the President had presented his own proposals in the form of a draft Parliamentary Bill. In these proposals, both the suggested devolution of powers from the centre and the twist sought to be given to them by the creation of a Second Chamber were designed more to perpetuate the ruling party in power than to find a lasting settlement to the ethnic problem. Even so, these proposals were repudiated by the President's own cabinet and party which untruthfully sought to pretend that they emanated from the Round Table Conference and not from the President."

Mr. N. Sanmugathasan, General Secretary of the Communist party, gave a press statement on the All Party Conference which was reported in *The Saturday Review*, an English language newspaper based in Jaffna, on 12th January as follows,

"The APC was expected to evolve a set of proposals which could be a viable alternative to the demand for a separate state of Eelam. What the President has proposed is simply an extension of local government but which is highly centralised and financially tied hand and foot to the centre. The proposed provincial councils do not have the right even to run a school or hospital or have jurisdiction over a court in their area. The whole point is that the government is not willing to recognise the right of self-determination of the Tamil people.

The representatives of the Tamil people have declared their willingness to accept any viable alternative to Eelam. They have also indicated that any genuine form of autonomy along the lines of Annexure 'C' to which President Jayewardene gave his assent when he went to New Delhi in November 1983 for the Commonwealth Leaders' Conference would be acceptable. Under these proposals, the Tamils can co-exist with the Sinhalese inside a single state but with regional autonomy and the right to run their own affairs in the Northern and Eastern Province. But the autonomy must be real ..."

This is the crucial factor, that, to provide any possibility of a solution to the present problems, the autonomy conferred must be real. An examination of the proposed legislation reveals that it is too far removed from conferring any real devolution of power to ever have' had any prospect of being acceptable to the Tamil people.

It is urged that immediate consideration be given to the provision of genuine regional autonomy. From conversations I had in February, 1985, with Tamils from different sectors of society it was plain that many still feel that real devolution of power would be an acceptable alternative to a separate state. However, the longer the passage of time which is allowed to elapse before effective regional autonomy is granted, the more likely it is that more and more Tamils will refuse to compromise upon the demand for a separate state.

[Note: Since the time of writing this section there have been many more meetings between the TULF and government representatives, and later between government representatives and the TULF and representatives of Tamil militant groups. Proposals and counter-proposals have been put forward, altered or rejected outright. At times the government of India has acted as intermediary. Acrimony, misunderstandings, unwillingness at times by both sides to listen or compromise, and disagreements within both groups as to the terms which are acceptable to their side, have not assisted the process. A peaceful solution on agreed terms seems no nearer now than it did in June 1985].

x) Government response to earlier recommendations that enquiries be held into various aspects of the communal disturbances of July 1983

As noted earlier, during the tragic and horrifying disturbances of the last week of July 1983 members of the police and armed forces had stood by and allowed attacks to be made on the Tamil people. Even worse, in some cases they had actively participated in the attacks. There had been a pattern to the violence, and in addition to the attacks made on civilians in cities and towns, Tamil political detainees held in Welikade prison had been massacred in circumstances raising serious questions, never since resolved, as to how such incidents could have occurred, on two separate occasions, in a top security gaol unless there had been complicity by those in a position of control.

Basic tenets of a civilised and democratic society, the rule of law, and the right of all citizens to equal protection before the law, are collapsing when the security forces cannot be relied upon by citizens of a minority group to ensure their physical safety, and when detainees are murdered while held in a state prison. All governments have a duty to protect their minorities, and to protect the persons held in detention. This protection was not afforded.

In circumstances such as these, in order that confidence might be restored, it was essential that independent, impartial enquiries be held and that the people responsible for the organisation of the attacks, those who participated in them, and the members of the security forces who had breached their duties, be identified and brought to account.

At the time of the first LAWASIA mission to Sri Lanka in August 1983, the government was indicating a clear intention to carry out thorough investigations. For instance, as noted earlier, in Parliament on August 4th 1983, Mr. Gamini Dissanayake, the Minister for Lands and Land Development and Minister of Mahaweli Development, said,

"...When matters like this happen, it is difficult to get the necessary evidence, but have no fear. This Government is going to reveal to this country the entire truth, warts and all even if it means that a part of the blame or the whole blame should fall on the government."

In the full text of the first LAWASIA report, as in other reports since made by different international human rights organisations, recommendations were made for the immediate institution of public enquiries by an independent and impartial body. It was important that the body appointed be independent of the security forces, and be one in the impartiality of which all Sri Lankans could have confidence. Prompt and full publication of the findings was urged, to be followed by the prosecution of all suspected offenders.

At the time of the second LAWASIA observer mission in February, 1985, no independent, impartial enquiries of the nature suggested had been carried out.

A magisterial enquiry had been conducted immediately after the prison massacres. As recorded earlier in the section on the Welikade murders, the magistrate returned verdicts of homicide upon all the deceased prisoners. Those who testified did not identify any of the persons responsible for the killings. The magistrate recommended that police enquiries be instigated. Inconclusive police enquiries followed. Despite the fact that these events had occurred in a top security gaol, and hence there was a limited number, both of offenders and of eye-witnesses, all identifiable and available, no charges had been laid against anyone for any of these murders at the time of my visit in February, 1985.

Concerning enquiries into the communal disturbances, information provided by Lieutenant-General D. Perera, the Sri Lankan High Commissioner in Canberra, is to the effect that police investigations have been made into 16,468 complaints registered after July, 1983. As a result of these enquiries 648 prosecutions have been filed. In 680 further cases enquiries have been almost finalised and the filing of prosecutions is imminent. In 7,378 cases enquiries are still pending, and in 7,762 cases there is no evidence available. In answer to queries as to the nature of the charges laid, Lieutenant-General Perera told me that, at the beginning of 1985, 30 charges had been laid for murder, the rest were for arson and looting.

The fact that these investigations have been made and charges laid is to be welcomed. However, in the circumstances, it was crucial that the enquiries should be made by a body independent of the security forces if confidence in the rule of law was to be re-established.

In February 1985 in response to my questions to government officials as to why the recommended public, independent enquiries had not been undertaken, the main answers I received were: that there are insufficient resources; Sri Lanka is not a rich country; there has been no time; it is not possible to obtain evidence showing who is responsible for the violence committed during the 1983 disturbances, either on the streets or in the prisons; people will not testify against each other, soldiers will not testify against soldiers and prisoners will not testify against prisoners. I was told that in any case it is not appropriate to instigate enquiries such as these when the government is involved in fighting a war.

Although it is appreciated that the task of the Sri Lankan government was at that time, and is still so today, one of immense difficulty, failures such as those outlined above have not assisted in the calming of tensions, and have certainly not assisted in the vital task of the maintenance of the rule of law, nor in persuading the Tamil people that their physical safety can, and will be, guaranteed by the present government.

[Concerning the necessity for impartial and independent enquiries see also III B vi regarding abuses carried out in relation to persons detained under the authority of the *Prevention of Terrorism Act*; regarding reprisal attacks by the security forces see III C below].

C. Reprisal attacks by members of the security forces on the civilian population of the north and east

As mentioned already, the personnel of the security forces, who are overwhelmingly Sinhalese, are, in the main, unable to speak the language of the people of the northern and parts of the eastern regions. They become increasingly fearful and hostile towards the Tamil population in these areas and, when unable to locate the militants who attack them, frequently carry out brutal reprisals — murder, rape, arson and looting — in retaliation upon unarmed civilians in the villages in the locality of the attacks.

The position of the young Sinhalese servicemen who are caught in this situation is not an enviable one. They do not wish to be sent to the troubled areas of the country where they are the targets of attack by militants whom they seldom can identify. They cannot communicate with, and get to know, the local inhabitants of the areas. They feel increasingly isolated, tense and fearful. Their task is undeniably unpleasant, dangerous and difficult. Many of them are killed or injured by an unseen enemy whilst attempting to perform their duties. In such circumstances the temptation to retaliate indiscriminately is an obvious one. Reliable reports clearly indicate that it is a reaction which has occurred frequently.

However, seeking to comprehend certain behaviour should not be confused with condonation. Despite the difficulties under which they are operating, the role of security forces in the disturbed areas of their own country is to maintain order. In a nation subscribing to the principles of the rule of law it is not open to the security forces to resort to unlawful and violent methods and to carry out reprisals against unarmed members of the population. As Sharvanada J. said in the *Velmurugu Case* (S.C. Application No. 74 of 1981, p.5), when considering the principles on which liability for infringement of fundamental rights is imputed to the state under the *Constitution*,

"If the State invests one of its officers or agencies with power which is capable of inflicting the deprivation complained of, it is bound by the exercise of such power even in abuse thereof; the official position makes the abuse effective to achieve flouting of the subject's fundamental rights. The State had endowed the officer with coercive power, and his exercise of its power, whether in conformity with or in disregard of fundamental rights, constitutes 'executive action'".

The government has an obligation to ensure that the security forces do not contravene the rule of law, and that its own citizens are protected.

It is appreciated that the government has appealed repeatedly for calm and restraint when militant attacks take place. In *The Island*, on December 15th, 1984, the Minister for National Security is reported to have asked, at a passing out parade of the Police Special Task Force, that they should "remember that in the course of their duties in putting down terrorism they were only fighting a group of their own misdirected citizens", and he said,

"You must be able to win the hearts of the people. To do so you must be thoroughly disciplined and courteous towards them. You must not only ensure the safety of your commanders but also those taken into your custody."

In *The Daily News*, on Monday, January 14th, 1985, the same Minister is reported to have urged security personnel to try winning the hearts of the people they come in contact with in the course of their duties, saying, "This is as important as winning the struggle against terrorism".

The Weekend, a Colombo based newspaper, reporting on a meeting held in Bulathsinhala on December 23rd, 1984, recorded the following statement by the President,

"We must win the hearts and minds of the people of the North. They have undergone some hardships because of the security operations and naturally they are bitter at the army. This must be remedied."

Nevertheless, the atrocities continue. I heard many horrifying accounts of the excesses committed by members of the security forces, and I was left in no doubt that reprisal attacks against unarmed Tamil civilians are both frequent and brutal. Amnesty International has documented very many of these incidents. So have other organisations. I include here just one account. It appeared in a statement published by the Civil Rights Movement of Sri Lanka in January, 1985,

"The security forces still retaliate against the civilian population after attacks by the militants. Several incidents have been brought to the attention of CRM. The instance of the incidents at Mannar on 4th December 1984 can be taken as one of the worst. An attack on a jeep which resulted in the death of one soldier and injury to several others had been followed, according to reliable reports, by a mass attack on civilians living within 3 to 4 miles of the incident, on the passsengers of buses plying on this road and on the staff of the Murunkan Post Office. The final death toll has been estimated at about 107.

Numerous other cases of arbitrary killing of civilians by the security forces have been also reported from Jaffna, Vavuniya and Mullaitivu districts. There have been other alleged incidents in Mannar as well, in which civilians including two members of Christian clergy have been killed."

The statement goes on to refer also to the increasing numbers of complaints that women have been sexually molested and raped by some members of the security forces in their search and arrest operations. Complaints of theft during these operations have been reported also.

Despite the frequency and the brutality of the reprisal attacks, as far as I could establish the severest penalty to date imposed upon any military personnel involved has been dismissal from the armed forces.

Information upon "collective punishments" was supplied to me by Lieutenant-General Perera. In this information two sets of incidents are listed. In one set, some Tamil militant attacks upon members of the security forces are recorded. In these instances it is stated that there was no over-reaction and military discipline remained firm. In the other set, members of the armed forces have been disciplined for their suspected involvement in retaliatory attacks upon civilians. The disciplinary action taken includes: the disbandment of 1 battalion; the discharge of 350 members of the armed forces; trial in military proceedings of 13 , and the sending of 1 soldier to gaol for three months.

From my conversations with people when I was in Sri Lanka in February 1985, it would appear that the public is very often not aware that such disciplinary action has been taken. It is recommended that this information be made common knowledge.

Though the fact that some disciplinary action has been taken is to be welcomed, again, in order for confidence to be restored, and justice to be seen to be done, it is necessary to appoint a body independent of the security forces and to conduct enquiries in public. It is then essential that dismissal be not the only sanction. Killings, rape and arson are extremely serious offences and they demand the application of the ordinary criminal law to their perpetrators.

Government explanations that it is impossible to identify those responsible, and hence to bring them before the criminal courts, cannot be accepted when no attempt has been made to institute independent and impartial enquiries into these instances. In this situation enquiries by the senior officers of those suspected to be involved are not an adequate response.

To the Tamil civilians in the northern and eastern regions, the current situation not unnaturally indicates that the government is unconcerned that its own forces are carrying out these indiscriminate reprisal attacks. They see this as yet a further indication that the government has, in effect, declared war upon the entire Tamil population, not just upon those engaged in violent activities. Naturally, this results in yet further disillusionment and gives strength to the feeling that only in a separate state will the physical safety of Tamil people be ensured.

D. Government actions indicating a commitment to human rights principles and a willingness to improve relationships with the Tamil people.

It should be noted that President Jayewardene's government has, since the UNP won the election in 1977, taken several steps which indicate a substantial commitment to the protection of human rights.

Under the leadership of the present government Sri Lanka, in June, 1980, acceded to the *International Covenant on Economic, Social and Cultural Rights* and the *International Covenant on Civil and Political Rights*. She also made a declaration under Article 41 of the latter recognising the Human Rights Committee as competent to hear inter-state complaints of violations. This government action, subjecting as it does the status of human rights within Sri Lanka to assessment in accordance with international norms is a most welcome and positive move. As yet Sri Lanka has not ratified the Optional Protocol which allows individual complaints. This would be desirable.

In 1982 the government acceded to the *International Convention on the Suppression and Punishment of the Crime of Apartheid* and the *International Convention on the Elimination of all Forms of Racial Discrimination*. Accession to this last Convention is particularly welcome. In the context of the country's ethnic problems, it indicates a desire on the part of the government to overcome tensions of this kind and to act in accordance with the Convention's precepts affirming, as they do, "the necessity of speedily eliminating racial discrimination throughout the world in all its forms and manifestations".

Racial discrimination is defined in the Convention as,

"any distinction, exclusion, restriction or preference based on race, colour, descent, or national or ethnic origin, which has the purpose or effect of nullifying or impairing the recognition, enjoyment or exercise, on an equal footing, of human rights and fundmental freedoms in the political, economic, social, cultural or any other field of public life".

Unfortunately, some of the government policies examined above indicate that these intentions have not yet been translated into practice in all areas.

The *1978 Constitution*, promulgated by the present government, contains a more comprehensive chapter on fundamental rights than did the *1972 Constitution* which it replaced. Chapter III enumerates the fundamental rights afforded constitutional protection. Many, but not all of the rights contained in the *International Covenant on Civil and Political Rights* are included. Protected are: freedom of thought, conscience and religion; freedom from torture or cruel, inhuman or degrading punishment; the right to equality and freedom from discrimination on the grounds of race, religion, language, caste, sex, political opinion or place of birth (the possibility of providing special protection for the advancement of women, children or disabled persons is preserved); freedom from arbitrary arrest, detention and punishment; prohibition of retro-active penal legislation, and freedom of speech, assembly, association, occupation and movement.

By Article 4(d) it is stated,

"the fundamental rights which are by the Constitution declared and recognised shall be respected, secured and advanced by all the organs of government, and shall not be abridged, restricted or denied, save in the manner and to the extent hereinafter provided."

Constitutional protection of rights such as these is commendable. Unfortunately, the government by certain of its legislative provisions, their modes of implementation, and some government operations outlined earlier, has failed to observe many of these constitutional provisions in a manner similar to its failure to observe some of the norms of international law.

Regrettably, the effectiveness of the protection afforded by Chapter III of the *Constitution* is diminished substantially by Article 15. This article allows restrictions to be placed on many of the protected rights. Restrictions may be made in the interests of national security, racial or religious harmony, national economy or public order, and the protection of public health or morality. No limitation, however, of the rights protected by Article 10, freedom of thought, conscience and religion, or Article 11, freedom from torture, cruel, inhuman or degrading punishment is permitted by Article 15.

A very valuable provision which this government has introduced is Article 126. This Article makes provision for the enforcement of the rights protected under Chapter III, giving to the Supreme Court the sole and exclusive jurisdiction to determine questions relating to the infringement, by executive or administrative action, of any fundamental right, or language right, protected by the *Constitution*. In President Jayewardene's words,

"An expeditious remedy for violation of fundamental rights is constitutionally guaranteed for the first time. That remedy can be sought from the highest court, whose independence and jurisdiction are entrenched in the Constitution." (Speech of the President at the inauguration of the Sixth LAWASIA Conference, Colombo, August 1979).

Article 126 is not uncommonly invoked but, again unfortunately, the effectiveness of the protection afforded here is restricted, in this case, by the limiting time constraints. It is necessary to invoke Article 126 within one month of the occurrence of the breach. This is not always possible. For instance, a detainee may have been assaulted while still in prison, and then remain in prison for more than one month after the assault, or it may be that upon release he or she is in no proper physical or mental condition to institute proceedings immediately.

In addition it should be noted that Article 27 of Chapter VI of the *Constitution* contains many of the provisions which receive protection under the *International Covenant on Economic, Social and Cultural Rights*. These are included as "directive principles of state policy and fundamental duties". They are not enforceable. Article 29 provides,

"The provisions of this Chapter do not confer or impose legal rights or obligaions, and are not enforceable in any court or tribunal. No question of inconsistency with such provisions shall be raised in any court or tribunal."

Further, Article 156 makes provision for the establishment of the Office of the Parliamentary Commissioner for Administration, or the Ombudsman. The duty of this officer is to investigate and report

"upon...allegations of the infringement of fundamental rights and other injustices by public officers and officers of public corporations, local authorities and other like institutions..."

The independence of the judiciary, a factor indispensable to any society which is to be governed in accordance with the rule of law, receives welcome and comprehensive protection under Chapter XV of the new *Constitution*. This is discussed more fully in the later sub-section on the judiciary, IV E. It is there observed, however, that no matter how impressive the guarantees provided by a country's constitution, ultimately they will be only as effective as those in the possession of power to implement them really wish them to be.

A significant step which this government has taken, and which has the potential to be of great value, is the support that it has given to the Human Rights Centre of the Sri Lanka Foundation. Mr. Harry Jayewardene, QC, the President's brother, is the Chairman of the Foundation. This organisation undertakes promotional and educational activities. While a protection role also would be desirable, within its confines the activities of the Centre have been beneficial. Its activities are covered in more detail in the sub-section immediately following.

Also encouraging is the continued and active presence of a number of effective and independent non-governmental organisations, for example, the Civil Rights Movement, the Centre for Society and Religion, the Movement for Inter-Racial Justice and Equality and other, similar groups. Such bodies, to the embarrassment of this and previous administrations, publicly express clear criticism of alleged government actions which threaten to breach the fundamental rights of the citizens.

Regarding the problem of Tamil grievances, from the outset the President expressed a willingness and a desire to deal with these. In its election manifesto the UNP made the following undertakings in 1977,

"UNITED NATIONAL PARTY
Problems of the Tamil-speaking people
The United National Party accepts the position that there are numerous problems confronting the Tamil-speaking people. The lack of a solution to their problems has made the Tamil-speaking people support even a movement for the creation of a separate State. In the interest of national integration and unity so necessary for the economic development of the whole country, the Party feels such problems should be solved without loss of time. The Party, when it comes to power, will take all possible steps to remedy their grievances in such fields as (1) Education (2) Colonisation (3) Use of the Tamil Language (4) Employment in the Public and Semi-public Corporations. We will summon an All Party Conference as stated earlier and implement its decisions."

On coming to power President Jayewardene encouraged Tamil participation in the process of government. Some of his ministers are Tamils. Today the Chief Justice is a Tamil, and there are Tamils in high positions in the public service.

Other steps taken by this government to ameliorate the grievances of the Tamil people were considered earlier. These include the conferral upon the Tamil language of the status of a national language, and the establishment in 1980 of District Development Councils, which were designed to provide a measure of regional autonomy. The purpose behind both innovations was to give recognition and effect to Tamil aspirations. These were commendable moves and it is regrettable that the manner of their implementation has resulted in a failure to achieve their aims.

At the 41st Session of the UN Commission on Human Rights, held in Geneva in February and March, 1985, Mr. Harry Jayewardene, QC, outlined measures which the government has taken to inculcate into members of the security forces a respect for human rights principles,

"The Government of Sri Lanka has done more than punish errant members of its security forces. It has taken positive measures to ensure discipline among service personnel. It has conducted programmes on Human Rights intended to inculcate a sense of respect for Human Rights among the members of the security forces. Government law officers have delivered a series of lectures on Human Rights to Army, Navy, Air Force and Police personnel. An organisation is being set up under the aegis of the Human Rights Centre of Sri Lanka and with the patronage of the President, the Prime Minister, the Chief Justice and the Leader of the Opposition for the promotion of Human Rights among the law enforcement agencies. The United Nations documents relating to law enforcement and Human Rights have been translated into the national languages for distribution to all members of the military and police services. The Government has enabled aggrieved parties to seek compensation for loss of property caused by the security forces in the course of their operations."

Such measures are to be welcomed and the government is to be commended for their instigation. Unfortunately, so far, they do not appear to have been successful in bringing to a halt the reprisal attacks which members of the security forces perpetrate on unarmed civilians.

E. Some examples of initiatives within Sri Lanka to re-establish discourse and trust between the different communities

From conversations with individuals from both communities it seems that amongst ordinary citizens there is still a willingness to try to understand and a sincere desire to achieve a solution to the ethnic conflict through moderation and compromise.

In fact a number of bodies, committees of concerned citizens and religious groups, have been taking steps to re-establish dialogue and trust between not only the Tamils and Sinhalese but among all communities. In the endeavour to achieve this aim some excellent programmes have been established. An exhaustive documentation of these initiatives will not be attempted here. Mention will be made of a few examples only.

A new organisation, the Bikkhu Organisation for Humanity, was formed by young Buddhist monks after they had witnessed the atrocities committed during the July 1983 disturbances. It operates only within Sri Lanka, and is committed to the preservation of the human rights of all persons regardless of class, creed or ethnic origin. Attempts are being made to establish dialogue with Tamil people of all persuasions. Importantly, the organisation is dedicated to the task of emphasising, amongst Buddhist monks themselves, the peaceful teachings of the Buddhist religion. The leaders of this new organisation wish to awaken their brethren to the fact that, consequent upon excessive Sinhala-Buddhist fervour, many injustices and injuries have been inflicted upon innocent people.

The Bikkhu Organisation for Humanity opposes the idea of separatism. It also opposes violence from any quarter, and all discriminatory practices. The organisers hope to create a climate in which the two sides can come together and reach mutual understanding. From this basis they feel it should be possible to find solutions to the present problems. The monks involved have organised a public seminar on the ethnic problem, and they produce, in Sinhala, a periodical bulletin on human rights matters. A letter, written by one of the monks and expressing friendship, understanding and concern towards Tamils in the northern province appeared in the April 6 1985 edition of the Jaffna newspaper, *The Saturday Review*.

Despite a lack of resources, which hampers the society's ability to engage more actively in many of the projects which it would like to pursue, this society is having success. I met two of its leaders. My impression is that they are gentle, articulate, sincere men, with a deep understanding of the current tensions and difficulties, and a real commitment to bringing about change. They told me that dialogue is being established with Tamil people, with people from other religions, and that the society is gaining support from an increasing number of young Buddhist priests, although opposition from older priests is encountered.

The society is an example of what can be done. With support it could do much more.

The International Centre for Ethnic Studies is another organisation which is taking positive steps to reduce racial tensions and to promote understanding between the different communal groups within Sri Lanka. It holds seminars, carries out research, and amongst its activities has produced television programmes designed to promote informed discussion about the country's current problems. Four programmes have been produced in the English language. They examine the complexities of a Sri Lankan national identity extending beyond ethnic identities. The grievances between the communities are looked at in some detail. Discussion is focused upon the sharing of national resources among people of all ethnic backgrounds. Land, education and employment receive the major emphasis. The final programme covers the topic of devolution of power and its implications for the future of Sri Lanka.

These programmes have been shown on television in Sri Lanka. The issues discussed are presented in a clear, factual and informative manner, in the setting of a discussion forum. Representatives from different backgrounds take part. Those to whom I spoke, who had seen the programmes, reacted very favourably to them. They felt that the programmes laid valuable ground-work from which discussions could continue on an enlightened basis. The Centre has prepared similar programmes in the Sinhalese language and is preparing Tamil programmes. The programmes are available as videos.

Initiatives such as this provide excellent groundwork for the development of ways of bringing about a peaceful resolution to the present problems. It is desirable that the maximum number of people be enabled to view the programmes, both at showings in community halls and at meetings as well as on prime-time television.

Another organisation of potentially great value has already been mentioned briefly. This is the Human Rights Centre of the Sri Lanka Foundation. This body undertakes promotional and educational activities. One of its achievements has been the creation and introduction of programmes within schools to propagate knowledge of the international human rights covenants.

A valuable project which the Centre is currently undertaking is the production of a commentary on the text of the *Universal Declaration of Human Rights*. This is being done from Buddhist, Hindu, Muslim, Christian and secular perspectives. The Centre hopes that such a commentary will be able to play a valuable role in fostering awareness of, and commitment to, the values enshrined in that Declaration. In a document produced by the Centre which briefly outlines the project it is stated,

"... In a plural society, such as ours, there are by definition different religious and cultural groups, and each of these groups has, again by definition, its own 'language' and its own symbols .... However, a common language for common values is essential if we are to live together with understanding, and the language of human rights offers to some extent such a language; it is not the language of one particular group; it can be understood by all, and does not offend the sensibilities of any group. It is on this common basis that society can be built anew in the present circumstances. .... human rights will be seen as, in a sense, part of one's own religion ... the implications for social behaviour ... are the same for all ... Here there is unity in spite of religious differences.

... A commentary must make it clear that the social harmony which is fostered by human rights does not demand the suppression of differences; what it does demand is the acceptance and observance of certain norms, so that differences do not lead to hostility and ultimately to a social behaviour which seeks to suppress differences."

Another organisation which is active in its attempt to promote communal harmony and to find solutions is MIRJE, the Movement for

Inter-Racial Justice and Equality. In January, 1985, this body issued a press statement deploring the resort to violence by both sides and urging a return to the negotiating table. The press release concluded that

"MIRJE must sadly point out that the only alternative to a political solution is further carnage, further loss of the democratic rights to which we have been accustomed, further brutalisation of our people and the strengthening of the authoritarian trends that are already evident in our society."

The Centre for Society and Religion is another very active organisation. Under its auspices many relevant books and papers have been published. The Centre also promotes and encourages discussion.

In Sri Lanka today there are many other religious organisations, organisations of concerned citizens and citizens' committees, which are involved in initiatives to bring about dialogue, understanding and reconciliation within the country. They number among their members many able, intelligent, perceptive and extremely dedicated people.

The very existence and activity of such people and organisations, and their many and different approaches and activities, is in itself a most encouraging sign. However, to enable the full benefit of these efforts to be reaped most of the organisations need positive assistance in forms which will enable them to develop their projects to maximum advantage and to reach large numbers of people in an effective manner.

Capital must be made of this willingness, enterprise, interest and commitment. Here the government has the obligation to take the lead and to set the stage upon which these initiatives may be utilised to their full potential.

IV

EROSIONS OF DEMOCRACY AND THE RULE OF LAW

Having reviewed the background factors and grievances which underlie the present tensions and escalating violence in Sri Lanka, it is pertinent to mention here other matters which are of concern to LAWASIA. These items are not specifically related to the ethnic troubles. They are, nevertheless, matters of considerable significance for they pose a threat to the rule of law and the principles of democracy, two values which Sri Lankans traditionally have clearly endorsed.

These matters are briefly outlined below. They include the 1978 Constitution and the powers which it confers on the President, amendments to the Constitution, changes to the electoral laws, proscription of opposition parties, threats to the independence of the judiciary, and the increasing numbers of acts of lawlessness which are allowed to occur without check by the law enforcement agencies.

A. The 1978 Constitution and the powers it confers on the President

In 1978 the new *Constitution* promulgated by the present government established a Presidential-style system. This *Constitution* confers very wide powers on the President. Article 30(1) provides that he is "the Head of the State, the Head of the Executive and of the Government, and the Commander-in-Chief of the Armed Forces." The Prime Minister, the Ministers and the Deputy Ministers are all appointed by the President (Articles 43, 44 and 46), and he has the power to remove them (Article 47).

Under Article 44(2) and (3) the President "may assign to himself any subject or function" and "may, at any time, change the assignment of subjects and functions and the composition of the Cabinet of Ministers". As of February, 1985, the President had assigned to himself the subjects and functions pertaining to the Ministry of Defence, the Ministry of Plan Implementation, the Ministry of Janata Estates Development, the Ministry of State Plantations, the Ministry of Higher Education and the Ministry of Power and Energy. (Hansard, 20th February, 1985).

The President may dissolve Parliament (Article 70). He appoints the Secretaries (i.e. permanent heads) to the Ministries (Article 52), and appoints the Attorney-General, the Heads of the Army, the Navy, the Air Force and the Police Force and all public officers required by the Constitution or other written law to be appointed by him (Article 54). The President also appoints the Chief Justice, the President of the Court of Appeal, and all the judges of the Supreme Court, the Court of Appeal and the High Court (Articles 107 and 111).

Thus, under the Constitution, the President is given extremely wide powers.

Article 42 does provide a safeguard, with its provision that the President shall be responsible to Parliament for the due exercise of his powers and duties. Nevertheless, the huge majority of government-party held parliamentary seats (140 out of 168, and, since the TULF ceased to occupy its seats, 140 out of 152 seats) renders this check on the President's power much less effective than might appear to be the case from a simple perusal of the Article. As a consequence of this overwhelming government majority the role which Parliament can play in terms of real and constructive discussion and review of executive action has been severely weakened. It is no longer a body functioning with the independence of the executive which the legislatures in democratic systems normally enjoy.

Furthermore, Article 35(1) provides that, for so long as he holds office as President,

"no proceedings shall be instituted or continued against him in any court or tribunal in respect of anything done or omitted to be done by him either in his official or private capacity".

The President has in his possesssion signed, undated letters of resignation of all the Members of Parliament of his party. Until these letters are either returned to their writers, or destroyed, the situation is clearly capable of the construction put upon it by Mr. Sarath Muttetuwegama MP (Communist Party), who, in the debate upon the continuation of the state of emergency held in Parliament on September 22, 1983, said,

"...we know one thing, that at the end of the day when the two-thirds majority is necessary the entire voting machine of the Government will be here. Whether they have heard the arguments, whether they are convinced of the arguments, or not, they will be here because if they are not here their letters of resignation will reach you tomorrow and they will cease to be Members of Parliament."

There is no reason to conclude that the President engineered this state of affairs, the various aspects of which have, in combination, given him such extensive powers. However, the net outcome is that there is today in Sri Lanka a dangerously large accumulation of power in the possession of one organ of government, the executive, and in the hands of one man, the President.

B. Amendments to the Constitution

Although the present Constitution has been in existence for only seven years it has been amended nine times. As has been observed already, it is never difficult for the present government to achieve the two-thirds majority vote which is required for constitutional amendments by Article 82(5).

Only the Third, Fourth and Sixth Amendments are relevant here. The Sixth Amendment has been fully covered in an earlier section, as has the fact that in the case of the passage of all these three Amendments the government complied with the formal requirements of the Constitution.

Also mentioned earlier was the point made to me by many Sri Lankans that, at the time of the passage of the Third and Fourth Amendments, the support for the UNP was declining and that, realistically, it could not have expected to have retained its large majority had a general election been held. The passage of the Amendments avoided the necessity for general elections. The terms of office of both the President, who received a vote of 52.9%, and the Parliament, were extended for a further six year period. The government maintained its massive majority in Parliament (140 out of 168 seats) by a vote of 54.6%.

The referendum to extend the life of the Parliament was conducted in a manner which was far from satisfactory. Briefly, the referendum was held under strictures which severely hampered the opposition campaign. Some opposition party members, notable amongst them being Mrs. Bandaranaike, leader of the SLFP, had been stripped of their civic rights, and thus deprived of the right to hold or campaign for public office or to support anyone else in that endeavour. A special Presidential Commission of Enquiry had been established under a law passed in 1978. This Commission had found Mrs. Bandaranaike and some of her followers guilty of "acts of political misuse or abuse of power". The acts in question had been carried out during her period in office. They had not been offences under any law at the time they were committed. This procedure is not used consistently by the present government to check the propriety of the behaviour of those currently in power. Its use in this instance deprived the SLFP, the party which has alternated in power with the UNP for many years, of its leadership.

I was told that at the time of the referendum other opposition party members and organisers were detained under the emergency regulations, and that some were subjected to short-term arrests and interference in the form of repeated questioning, the timing of which strongly suggested an attempt to hamper the opposition campaign. SLFP headquarters were raided and party documents, including membership lists, were seized.

The referendum was held under emergency regulations, although it seems that immediately prior to the referendum the Minister of State had indicated that conditions were once again normal and the state of emergency would be lifted before the election. Under the emergency regulations some opposition papers were banned, some opposition presses were sealed, and opposition leaflets outlining the constitutional issues raised by the referendum were seized. This hindered the opposition in its bid to put the real issues before the electorate.

The law concerning poster display was breached by the ruling party and no sanctions followed the breaches. Posters indicating support for the YES vote were placed in locations prohibited to posters, and were allowed to remain in position. Complaints to the police were ineffective.

The polling itself was marred by the harrassment of electoral officers, candidates and voters. There was also impersonation of voters. Brief mention of the unsatisfactory conduct of the Referendum has been made already. A statement by the Civil Rights Movement of Sri Lanka, put out at the time, concluded that the referendum may not have been "free and fair".

Despite calls for the appointment of a commission of enquiry into the election, as far as I was able to ascertain as at February 1985 an enquiry has not been held. Those who intimidated voters and presiding officers at polling stations, and those who breached the electoral laws have not been brought before the courts.

C. Changes in electoral laws

The Ceylon (Parliamentary Elections) Order-in-Council 1946 has been recently amended by Act No.36 of 1984. Until the time of the 1981 Jaffna District Development Council elections at which blatant irregulaties occurred, elections in Sri Lanka had always been conducted openly and honestly. On no occasion had there been any ground upon which the victory of a political party at an election could have been thrown into doubt. However, the irregularities which have now taken place, without check, indicate that the situation is deteriorating.

Among the provisions of the new Act which give rise to concern are the fact that henceforth a result may be declared even if ballot boxes are missing. An "information", which need not be in writing, that it is not possible to commence or continue a poll due to "the occurrence of events of such a nature", described as a "disturbance" in the marginal note, is conclusive of the existence of those events (Section 47A). Once an information has been made, counting can commence without the receipt of the ballot boxes from the polling station at which a "disturbance" has been reported, and the result can be declared without these votes being counted (Section 48).

The effect of this will be to dis-enfranchise those voters whose votes are in the ballot boxes which do not reach the counting station, and also to dis-enfranchise those who cannot vote due to the occurrence of "events of such a nature". In effect the legislation concedes, by making provision for them, that election irregularities will continue to be a feature of Sri Lankan life. This is a particularly disquieting development when, until so very recently, election irregularities were minimal and never of a serious nature.

The procedures which the new legislation establishes for the counting of votes and the declaration of winning candidates in circumstances where "disturbances" have occurred enable severe erosion of principles whose maintenance is essential if a truly democratic system is to survive.

D. Proscription of opposition parties

As mentioned already, from time to time opposition parties have been proscribed and some of their members imprisoned. Sometimes these detainees have been held incommunicado, without access to either lawyers or relatives, amidst government allegations of the parties' complicity in various suspected plots. So far no substantive evidence has been produced to support such allegations and no charges have been laid. Three leftist parties, the JVP (Janatha Vimukthi Peramuna), the NSSP (Nava Samasamaja Party) and the Communist Party were proscribed after the July 1983 disturbances amidst government allegations that they had been involved in plots to destabilise the country and overthrow the government. No evidence of such activities was ever produced. As far as I was able to ascertain, those imprisoned had all been released by the end of 1983 and no charges were laid against any of the detainees. The proscription of the first 2 parties was lifted, but, in early 1985, the JVP remains proscribed.

The use of proscription orders which immobilise opposition parties in circumstances where no evidence is produced to substantiate the allegations which are the justification for that proscription, and when people are nevertheless held in detention for weeks and months at a time, gives rise to serious concern about the value accorded by the present government to the right to political freedom. Such use of proscription orders can be turned into an instrument whereby the government seeks to remain in power at whatever cost.

Disquieting also is the fact that a challenge to the proscription of the JVP was brought in the Supreme Court, and the court held that, as the proscription order had been made by the President under the emergency regulations it was beyond challenge in the courts (Case No.107/84, Supreme Court). I was told that other, similar findings have been made, based upon the interpretation given to Article 35 of the Constitution. This is the Article which confers upon the President immunity from suit. Such findings have extremely serious ramifications, removing as they do Presidential orders from any possibility of a challenge for illegality.

When I was in Sri Lanka in February, 1985, the JVP was still the only party proscribed. I heard from government members allegations that there was ample evidence to show that this party is involved with the militants in a marxist plot to overthrow the government. There are also statements by the government to the effect that the JVP will use violence to achieve its ends.

Posters have appeared in public places depicting a coalition of the Tamil militant movements, the JVP and the Soviet Union, and a booklet "The Truth About Ealam Terrorists", in which the JVP is linked to Eelamism, is alleged by the JVP to have been printed at the government press and to have been given wide distribution.

At the time of my visit I was told that 23 JVP party supporters, whose names were given to me, were held in detention under the authority of the *Prevention of Terrorism Act*. As far as I could ascertain no charges had been laid against any of these people. Quite a few of the people to whom I spoke in February, 1985, expressed the view that the JVP is currently an opposition party which the government regards as a serious potential threat to its own position. This is because, before its proscription, the JVP was said to be emerging as a strong force. It attracts students and the younger voters. Hence the suggestion was that the government continued the proscription of this party more through fear of its potential support base than for the reason that there is any truth in the various charges.

The JVP did in the past resort to the use of violence. It was the organiser of an abortive, but violent, attempted insurrection in April 1971. As a result it was proscribed by Mrs. Bandaranaike's government from 1971 onwards. When President Jayewardene came to power in 1977 he lifted the ban. Since 1977 the party has stated its intention to take part in the democratic process. It has actively participated in elections. The party is now underground once more. Many people to whom I spoke said that they seriously doubted any links between it and the militant Tamil groups. Further, I was told that the openly stated policy of the party has always been one of opposition to the idea of a separate state.

Whatever the position may be, innuendo, proscription and attacks upon a rival political party, in the media and other publications, are no substitute for the substantiation of the government allegations by the production of evidence, or, if there is not in fact evidence of their truth, the dropping of the suggestions of such activities and the measures taken allegedly because of them.

E. Threats to the independence of the judiciary

The independence of the judiciary, an essential and pivotal feature to the continuation of a free and fair society conducted under the rule of law, is well provided for in Sri Lanka under the terms of the 1978 Constitution. The Preamble refers to the "immutable republican principles of representative democracy" and assures to "all peoples freedom, equality, justice, fundamental human rights and the independence of the judiciary as the intangible heritage that guarantees the dignity and well-being of succeeding generations..."

Article 107 governs the appointment and removal of judges of the Supreme Court and Court of Appeal. The appointments are made by the President, the judges hold office "during good behaviour", and shall not be removed except by the President after an address for removal made by Parliament, introduced by not less than a third of its members and supported by a majority of the total Members of Parliament, including those not present. By Article 108 judges' salaries are to be determined by Parliament and may not be reduced for any judge during that judge's term of office.

The judges of the High Court are appointed by the President and he has the power to terminate their appointments on the recommendation of the Judicial Service Commission (Article 111). The Judicial Service Commission consists of the Chief Justice, who is its chairman, and two judges of the Supreme Court appointed by the President. The President may, for cause, remove any member of the Commission (Article 112). The appointment, transfer, dismissal and disciplinary control of judicial officers (not including judges of the Supreme Court, Court of Appeal or High Court) is vested in the Commission (Article 114).

Article 116 provides that every judge shall exercise and perform his powers and functions without being subject to any direction or other interference, and that every person who, without legal authority, interferes or attempts to interfere with the exercise or performance of the judicial power or functions of any judge shall be guilty of an offence.

The constitutional safeguards securing the independence of the judiciary within Sri Lanka are excellent provisions. Despite them, however, the independence of the judiciary within that country has, in fact, been threatened more than once by incidents occurring in recent years. Constitutional guarantees depend for their effectiveness on a determination by those with substantial power under the Constitution that the guarantees be given force. As already noted, under the Sri Lankan Constitution substantial powers are vested in the President.

The transitional provisions of the 1978 Constitution, provided that

"all judges of the Supreme Court and the High Courts...holding office on the day immediately before the commencement of the Constitution shall, on the commencement of the Constitution, cease to hold office" (Article 163).

This gave the present government the opportunity, which it took, to effectively remove a number of judges from the former court by not re-appointing them and, instead, to appoint others to positions on the newly established Supreme Court. Many lawyers in Sri Lanka saw the changes thus made to have been politically motivated. The taking of such action meant that the government was able to avoid the effect of the constitutional safeguards to secure the tenure of the judiciary.

At the inauguration of the new Supreme Court the Chief Justice remarked,

"We have gathered together to usher in the New Supreme Court in the traditional manner known to Bench and Bar. I and my brothers have been members of the Old Supreme Court and would have wished for it an honourable demise and a decent burial, but that was not to be. Words have been uttered and aspersions cast in another place which seemingly affect its hallowed name. What more is in store I do not know."

More has been in store. In two cases since 1982 members of the police force have been promoted after having been found by the Supreme Court to have acted unlawfully. In each case the Supreme Court had heard complaints brought against the police officers concerned, under Article 126. As already noted, Article 126 gives to the Supreme Court sole and exclusive jurisdiction to determine questions relating to the infringement, by executive or administrative action, of any fundamental right protected by the Constitution.

The complaint made in the first case concerned the seizure by a Superintendent of Police, Mr. P. Udagampola, of 20,000 pamphlets put out by an organisation called Pavidi Handa (Voice of The Clergy). The pamphlets expressed opposition to the referendum to extend the life of Parliament. The Rev. Dharamitipola Ratanasara, the secretary of the organisation, brought an action under Article 126, alleging that this seizure infringed his fundamental right to freedom of speech and expression. In February, 1983, the Supreme Court handed down judgment, unanimously finding in the applicant's favour, and awarding damages and costs against the Superintendent. In March it was announced by the government that the Superintendent was to be promoted, and that the costs and damages would be paid by the State. It was reported in Colombo newspapers at the time that this action was taken to ensure that "public officers should do their jobs and follow orders without fear of consequences from adverse court decisions".

The complaint in the second case arose out of an incident occurring in March, 1983, during a demonstration on the occasion of International Women's Day. A press photographer was apprehended and taken to a police station. Mrs. Vivienne Goonewardene, a former Member of Parliament, went to enquire about the photographer. She was arrested, and alleged that she was assaulted while in the police station. She, too, brought an action under Article 126. The court found the arrest to have been unlawful, and Mrs. Goonewardene was awarded damages. As regards the assault charge, the court found itself unable to reach a decision due to the time constraints imposed by the *Constitution*. It recommended that the police investigate this charge. Judgment was handed down on June 8th.

On June 9th the promotion of the officer concerned, Mr. Ganeshanathan, a sub-inspector of the Kollupitiya Police, was announced by a senior member of the force. An official communiqué stated this promotion was "for the work done ... in dispersing a procession conducted by Mrs. Vivienne Goonewardene on 8.3.1983".

Two days later, the houses of the 3 Supreme Court judges who had delivered the judgment in the Goonewardene case were surrounded by rowdy mobs shouting obscenities and creating disturbances. In fact, one of the judges had recently moved, and his former house was surrounded by mistake. Placards carried referred to the judgment. No-one was hurt, but it was an unpleasant and frightening experience for the judges and their families. All attempts by the judges to obtain the assistance of the police proved futile.

An editorial in *The Island*, on 13th June, 1983, stated,

"There is proof that the demonstrators had been brought in buses. The authorities must initiate an immediate enquiry to ascertain who was responsible for this demonstration and why the police failed to respond .... If the judges of the Supreme Court cannot receive immediate protection from vulgar mobs what chance will the ordinary citizen stand?"

At the time claims for responsibility for these occurrences were made publicly by an alleged organiser. The mobs had arrived at the scene in public transport buses, and the evidence indicates that it was an organised, not a spontaneous, demonstration. Further, a state of emergency had been declared at the time, and the emergency regulations give to the government wide powers to control demonstrations. Nevertheless, as far as I have been able to ascertain, no one has been found to be responsible for the organisation of this event, nor have the government-owned buses in which the demonstrators had travelled to the scene of the demonstrations, been traced.

Such a situation neither protects the independence of the judiciary nor

serves to re-inforce, in the minds of the citizens of the country, a belief
that the rule of law will be respected and obseved.

Twice recently allegations of impropriety in the behaviour of judges
of the Supreme Court have been made. These allegations have been
considered by Select Committees of Parliament set up for the purpose.
The first such allegation was made in October 1982 by Mr. K.C.E.
de Alwis. Mr. de Alwis, a member of the Special Presidential
Commission of Enquiry which had investigated allegations against, *inter
alia*, Mrs. Bandaranaike, had himself been the subject of allegations of
impropriety. In his case they were allegations of impropriety in the
course of carrying out his duties as a member of the Commission. These
allegations had been heard by the Supreme Court. Two of the three
judges, Colin Thomé J. and Wimalaratne J., found that Mr. de Alwis
had been guilty of misconduct. Mr. de Alwis petitioned the President,
alleging that the two judges in question were biased against him, and
that some of the pleadings presented on behalf of the petition had been
prepared in the chambers of one of the judges, Percy Colin Thomé J.
Mr. Justice Colin Thomé has handed down several decisions which have
not pleased the executive government. He was one of the judges in both
the *Goonewardene case*, and the *Pavidi Handa case*. Mr. Justice
Wimalaratne was also one of the judges in the *Pavidi Handa case*.

The decision to establish a Parliamentary Select Committee was taken
in early March, 1983. The Committee tabled its report in July 1984. It
found that the allegations of bias and improper motive were unfounded,
but criticised the decision reached in the case in question.

The second allegations of misbehaviour concerned a prize-giving
speech made by the then Chief Justice, Neville Samarakoon, at the
Sinnathuray Commercial Tutory on March 14, 1984. Some government
members thought the speech too political. It was critical of some of the
policies of the executive government and of the President. On 3rd April
1984, the Prime Minister, Mr. R. Premadasa, moved a motion in
Parliament, which was passed, for the appointment of a Parliamentary
Select Committee to enquire into, and report upon, the propriety of the
Chief Justice's conduct in making the speech.

The government party members of the Committee found that the Chief
Justice had, by making a speech parts of which could be considered to
be politically controversial, behaved in a manner not befitting the holder
of the office of Chief Justice. They recommended that further steps be
taken. The opposition party members dissented from this finding,
exonerated the Chief Justice, and recommended that no further action
be taken.

On September 5th one-third of the Members of Parliament gave notice
of a resolution to present an address to the President for the removal
of the Chief Justice from his office. A second Select Committee of
Parliament was set up. Members were nominated by the Speaker, and

the Chief Justice was asked to show cause why he should not be removed from office. Before the deliberations of the Committee were complete and its report presented to Parliament the term of office of the Chief Justice had expired and he had retired.

The government party members of the Committee, the majority, found that the Chief Justice had broken a convention, but that his conduct did not amount to "misbehaviour" under Article 107(2). Mr. Nadesan, QC, counsel for the Chief Justice, and others, have questioned both the existence and the origin of the alleged convention. The minority members (the members from parties other than the UNP) dissented from the view that the Chief Justice had breached a convention and exonerated the Chief Justice. These members also thought that the matter should not have been dealt with by a Parliamentary Committee.

Many people expressed to me a concern that, taking into account the background in both cases, i.e. judgments delivered of which the executive disapproved, and statements made that were critical of the executive, the bringing of the judges before a Select Committee of Parliament was intended as a clear indication to the judiciary that they are subordinate to, and not independent of, the executive and the legislature. For reasons already mentioned, in the present circumstances in Sri Lanka, the Parliament does not have the independence from the executive generally enjoyed by legislatures in democratic systems.

I heard many expressions of concern that it is becoming more and more difficult for judges of the Supreme Court to impartially and fearlessly uphold the rule of law in circumstances where this would mean a conflict with the interests of those in political power.

Without an independent judiciary democracy cannot survive for long. In Blackstone's words,

"In this distinct and separate existence of the judicial power in a peculiar body of men, nominated indeed, but not removable at pleasure, by the Crown, consists one main preservative of the public liberty; which cannot subsist long in any state, unless the administration of common justice be in some degree separated both from the legislative and also from the executive power".
(*Blackstone's Commentaries Vol 1*, (7th ed.) at p 269.)

Sadly, it is difficult in the present circumstances to reach any conclusion other than that the independence of the judiciary is under threat in Sri Lanka today.

F. Other incidents which have tended to encourage lawlessness.

In addition to the events already mentioned in which lawlessness has been allowed to occur without check by the law enforcement agencies, there have been other incidents which have not been attended to thus far.

These include several occasions of attacks by organised mobs upon pickets and demonstrators. Such attacks occurred, for example, during the January 1980 demonstrations which were held to protest at a government decision to reduce the number of holidays which workers had previously enjoyed. In June 1980, demonstrators preparing for the general strike were attacked. The police did not provide protection in either case.

Meetings held by the opposition parties have been disrupted by mobs. Religious meetings have been similarly disturbed. Often police protection is not forthcoming. In some cases it has not been possible to hold proposed meetings at all because of acts of violence. This happened to a proposed meeting of Buddhist and Christian Clergy organised by the Pavidi Handa (Voice of The Clergy) in December, 1982, at Gampaha.

In addition women strikers and demonstrators are alleged to have been assaulted both by police and violent civilians. An example is the brutal attack upon trainee teachers demonstrating at the Maharagama Training College in June 1980.

Attacks by organised mobs occur not infrequently in Sri Lanka. There are available for hire, for the purpose of intimidating others, persons known as *goondas* or hooligans and thugs. Many people told me that different political parties, and other groups, hire contingents of *goondas* to serve their own purposes, and arrange for them to be transported to the places where they wish them to be active.

Goondas undoubtedly were present in large numbers in the July 1983, disturbances. They were present also in the June 1983 attacks on the houses of the Supreme Court judges, and have been employed in many other disturbances in Sri Lanka in recent years, for instance in the violence at the time of the District Development Council elections in Jaffna in 1981.

I heard reliable reports to the effect that, since 1977, university students on 7 campuses have been attacked by organised mobs coming in from outside the universities. In some cases the police are alleged not only to have failed to provide protection but to have actively participated in the attacks.

In July and August 1977, serious post-electoral and communal violence occurred. Threats, assaults, thefts, murder and arson were so prevalant that an official committee of enquiry was appointed to carry out an investigation into the events surrounding the election, and the Sansoni Commission was appointed to investigate the later communal violence. The first committee's report was submitted to the government but was never made available to the public.

The Sansoni Commission documented cases of assault, theft and arson both committed in the presence of police who stood by, and cases of assault by the police themselves. Any actions taken by the government in response to the Commissions finding have not been made public.

In 1982 an Indemnity Act (Act No.20 1982) was passed,

"with a view to restrict legal proceedings against Ministers, Deputy Ministers, or any person holding office in the government in any capacity, whether naval, military, police or civil, in respect of acts done during the period 1st August, 1977 to 31st August, 1977."

Such legislation inevitably gives rise to the impression that the government has condoned any breaches of the law which may have been committed by these people.

The fact that acts of violence are an increasingly common occurrence within Sri Lanka gives rise to serious concern. This concern must be the greater when the number of incidents in which the police fail to check the violence, and in which it is reported that they participate themselves, are taken into consideration. Since the perpetrators and organisers of disturbances such as those outlined above are not apprehended and brought before the courts, lawlessness and intimidating behaviour carried out by organised mobs is becoming more and more prevalent. Prevalent too, in the minds of many to whom I spoke in February 1985, is the impression that it is behaviour which the government either condones or is powerless to check.

V

CONCLUDING COMMENTS

The following conclusions and suggestions are presented tentatively, and solely with the intention to offer a positive contribution. Two brief missions to a country amounts to far too short a time to enable the formation of anything like a comprehensive understanding of all the underlying factors behind any crisis, particularly in a country with such a complex and rich fabric of history and composition of cultures, races and religions as Sri Lanka possesses. In these circumstances, it seems presumptuous to even attempt to make suggestions. However, it is possible that there are certain advantages in an outside viewpoint, notably the perspective which some distance from the problems may provide. It is in this spirit that this final section is written.

Although it has been necessary to note areas where government action has made severe inroads upon the principles of democracy and the rule of law, it is also the case that the present government has taken several steps which indicate a commitment to the protection of human rights.

Similarly, although acts of violence and atrocities have been committed by members of each community against the other, there have been also many acts of friendship and even heroism from people of one community to those of the other. Further, counter-balanced against inflammatory racist propaganda and the stirring up of antagonism between the two groups, must be placed the very considerable efforts which some bodies have made towards the establishment of communication, understanding and reconciliation.

The tragedy of the present situation of erosion of democratic values, weakening of the authority of the rule of law, perpetration of violence, and provocation of racial antagonism is highlighted when seen against the background of the country's exceptional assets. While the *per capita* income of the country is low, Sri Lanka possesses the essential resources to be successful. The population is highly literate (there is a more than 85% literacy rate amongst adults), life expectancy is 69 years at birth, and there is a low infant mortality rate (37.7 per thousand).

Sri Lanka has a long-established civilisation, a rich and varied culture, a tradition of democratic government, freedom of speech and respect for the rule of law, and, the present problems notwithstanding, a charming, friendly and overwhelmingly hospitable people. In addition Sri Lanka enjoys a good climate and physically is truly a tropical paradise. The country is remarkably beautiful with glorious palm-fringed beaches, large areas of forests, fertile lands, abundant farming and fishing, productive plantations, many historical monuments of great interest and antiquity, attractive villages, and cool and majestic mountain areas.

Tragically, much of her quality of life and many of her assets and the achievements of which she can be justifiably proud are now under threat.

For reasons stated in the body of this report the government must bear responsibility for many of the trends which recently have eroded the democratic system and shaken the authority of the rule of law.

It is appreciated that the task of the Sri Lankan government has been one of immense difficulty. So, also, is the position of the security forces. Further, as instanced on several occasions in the body of the report, different communities within Sri Lankan society now have very real fears and cause for deep resentments against other sectors of the society. It is also appreciated that the government has an obligation to control groups which are resorting to violent means to achieve their aims.

The use of violent tactics by the militant groups has caused a great deal of tension and resentment throughout the country. Further, this use of violence, the terrorising of those who hold different views, the destruction of property, the killing and maiming of members of the armed forces, and sadly, very recently the killing of Sinhalese civilians, must be condemned. Such actions breach the fundamental rights of all those affected. These acts of violence, coupled with the kind of coverage which they have received in the local Sri Lankan media and in publications issuing from government sources, have contributed in no small measure to the occurrence of some of the recent extreme reactions exhibited both by the security forces and by sectors of the general population against the Tamil people.

However, it must be remembered that unarmed Tamil civilians were the victims of communal violence in Sri Lanka long before the resort to violence by the militant youth, and long before the demand for a separate state had been articulated. For many years the Tamil people did not counter-attack despite several outbursts of communal violence directed against them and even though hundreds of Tamils have been killed, many more hundreds injured, and they have suffered immensely in terms of dislocation, property damage and hardship. Further, for decades Tamil leaders have participated in negotiations with the governments of the day, only to be disappointed, on several occasions, by the failure of those governments to implement either the agreements which had been reached, or the concessions which had been granted. Even today most Tamils in Sri Lanka do not resort to violence.

This assessment of the Tamil situation is not a justification for the militants' current resort to violent methods, and, as noted, governments have an obligation to take action against the perpetrators of violence.

Bearing in mind all the factors considered so far, at this point there would seem to be two major possible approaches which can be pursued. The first is to continue the policy currently being followed: to achieve desired ends by domination and coercion.

To take violent measures to control the perpetrators of violent methods is a comprehensible, instinctive response. But a circular pattern is thereby set in motion, and violence begets violence. This is precisely the type of instinctive "eye for an eye, tooth for a tooth" response that civilised society — in its establishment of legal systems — has sought to transcend and relegate to the level of an historical anachronism. A long-term solution will be achieved only through negotiation and removal of the grievances which underlie the Tamil militant movement.

As observed earlier, there is ample evidence that the strong legislative, administrative and military measures used so far by the government in its attempts to deal with the movement towards separatism and militancy have not worked. Instead, they have led to the increasing support which is now being given to the militant groups by a Tamil population which is becoming ever-more beleaguered and fearful even for its own physical security.

Victory by either side, achieved as a result of coercion, will only set the stage for later retaliation and a future replete with yet further atrocities.

At the time of writing this section, in the latter part of May 1985, accounts of two major outbreaks of violence have just been broadcast in Australia. In one incident it is alleged that, after an attack made upon the armed forces by militants, in which an officer and several men were killed, soldiers at Valvettithurai and Point Pedro killed approximately 100 Tamil civilians in reprisal. The other incident is an apparent reprisal to these events said to have been made by Tamil militants who entered the ancient, holy, predominantly Sinhalese city of Anuradhapura and opened fire on civilians there. As mentioned already, over 150 persons are reported to have been killed, including people who were at the Sri Maha Bodhi shrine. Hundreds more are reported injured. Further reprisal attacks have already followed upon these two dreadful atrocities. Whether or not the reports reflect the true nature of these attacks, what is clear is that many unarmed people who were in no way involved in the current hostilities, have just met a violent death. Many more have been seriously injured, and hundreds have been subjected to terrible fear, dislocation, suffering and loss.

This is an indication of how violence can, and in fact has, spiralled to an alarming extent.

If a solution by sheer force and coercion continues to be the approach selected, it is surely obvious that indiscriminate killings and acts of terror and inhumanity will increase even further. In these circumstances, for many innocent people death, anguish, and dreadful injuries become inevitable. Escalating violence must eventually reach the stage where there is a total collapse of normal civilised society.

The second possible approach is the method of negotiation.

In any negotiations which are held, the ability of the participants to carry with them the members of their communities is clearly of the utmost importance. Many government members told me that they felt the TULF party no longer commanded the support of the Tamil people of the north, and that it is therefore pointless to attempt to negotiate with the party leaders. These government members also stated that there is in fact no one who can claim to represent the Tamil people, and that hence negotiation is not possible.

Mr. Amirthalingam, leader of the TULF party, himself feels that the Tamil representation at the negotiations must extend beyond the leaders of the TULF. Indeed, he thinks it essential that negotiations be conducted between the government and a combined group of Tamil leaders if any real agreement is to be reached and to work.

It is the responsibility of the Tamil people to nominate the persons who can truly represent them. This step must be taken first.

Once this has been done it is vital that the government be prepared to negotiate with those chosen to represent the Tamil people, even if the selected representatives do include persons who profess strong support for separatism.

[Note: Since this report was completed government representatives have been prepared to meet, and have met and held discussions with, leaders of Tamil militant groups.]

In discussions with Lieutenant-General Perera, the Sri Lankan High Commissioner in Canberra, he told me that statements which have emerged from the recent talks held between the President of Sri Lanka and the Prime Minister of India in early June, 1985, are to the effect that the President is willing to grant devolution of power to the northern and eastern regions of the country and that the President hopes, by this means, to enable a climate of peace to be re-established in those areas, in order that those who have fled to the state of Tamil Nadu are enabled to return to their homes and resume a normal life there. Lieutenant-General Perera added that the President has indicated a desire that, as soon as circumstances permit, elections be held in the north and east to fill the parliamentary seats currently left vacant by the TULF members, and to fill the positions on those district councils in the north and east whose members have all resigned.

Lieutenant-General Perera told me that the President has stated that he is ready to discuss the matter of devolution of power with anyone at any time. The President has also reiterated the offer of an amnesty to all militants who do lay down their arms. These latest expressions of willingness to negotiate are to be welcomed most strongly. At this time it is absolutely essential that the SLFP, and other factions and groups, render assistance and give positive encouragement to the steps towards a political solution. At this stage it is crucial that the interests of the country as a whole be put before self-interested political rivalry.

In any negotiations which are held certain additional factors will have to be given recognition.

Account must be taken of the very real fears of the Tamils in Sri Lanka both regarding their physical security and their inability to rely upon the implementation of promises made by succeeding Sinhala-dominated governments. Nothing short of real devolution of power will now suffice. In order for Tamils to believe that any agreement reached will have any value, there must be clear provision made for the guarantee of its implementation by a body that is neutral and independent.

The negotiations must also make due account for the fears, clearly apparent amongst many Sinhalese, concerning their position as a minority in the region. As noted earlier, they number only 12,000,000 in all, whereas, twenty miles away across the water lie the closest shores of the state of Tamil Nadu in southern India where over 50,000,000 Tamils reside. As Paul Seighart observed, in the report which he made for the ICJ after his visit to Sri Lanka in January 1984, many Sinhalese see the Tamils who live in Sri Lanka as a kind of advance-guard for an invasion by the millions residing in southern India. Further, Sinhalese nationalism and its identification in the minds of many with the preservation of Buddhism are also highly significant factors. They must be taken into account when solutions are being canvassed.

For both these reasons, and because there is a natural desire that the whole island should remain united, the Sinhalese see a separate state as spelling catastrophe for them. They regard any form of federalism with only slightly less trepidation. In February 1985, I spoke to many Sinhalese who were extremely apprehensive about the role which India might play in Sri Lanka as a consequence of the current tensions, and about the role she may play in the future if a federal state were the solution selected.

Although the Indian government has repeatedly given assurances that no invasion will take place, such fears, once generated, are not easily dislodged. For this reason it is essential that any role which India might be called upon to play as an intermediary be carefully structured so that the Sinhalese are reassured as much as is possible on this point. It may be that consideration should be given here to the possibility of other independent intermediaries.

It is important that the government take the lead in the initiation of measures to re-establish calm and to set the stage upon which real dialogue is enabled to take place.

The evidence indicates that the current situation of violence and ethnic tensions within Sri Lanka is one which wise statesmanship could have avoided. Unfortunately, instead, steps have been taken to secure short-term political advantage and this practice still continues. Succeeding governments, political parties in opposition and other powerful factions have all been guilty of these tactics. Over the years there has been also a failure by those with influence and power to make a genuine commitment to find, and implement, measures to resolve the different problems and de-escalate the tensions. This combination has resulted in the tragic consequences which are now being visited upon the country.

Clearly, the development of the current situation cannot be laid at the door of the present government alone. Many other parties and factions have played a part. However, precisely because it is the government now in power it is imperative that it be the body to take the initiative to establish the conditions within which a solution through negotiation is possible. This is likely to involve some anxious transitions. There may be difficulty in arriving at the re-orientation required to seriously consider, develop and implement new approaches. These difficulties are very real but, unless the government is content, by design or default, to pursue a policy leading to great suffering, it is now essential that it act on measures hitherto considered unacceptable.

A basic requirement for effective negotiations is that all current attempts to impose a resolution by violence and coercion should be immediately halted. Since the attacks made upon civilians by the members of the security forces have contributed, in no small measure, to the escalation of violence, hostilities, tensions, and alienation of the Tamil people in the northern and eastern regions, it will be crucial, if the forces are to remain in these areas after a halt to armed violence is called, that totally effective control and restraint be imposed upon them. It will then be incumbent upon the Tamil militants also to observe the halt to hostilities absolutely.

There are some measures which it would be possible for the government to implement fairly swiftly and without great difficulty. It would assist greatly in the calming of tensions, and would provide a most welcome government initiative, if these were to be undertaken without delay. Such steps would include the suspension of the colonisation programme, the repeal of the Sixth Amendment and the encouragement of TULF members to participate once more in the parliamentary process.

It is urged that those emergency regulations and the sections of *The Prevention of Terrorism Act* which result in a breach by Sri Lanka of her obligations under *The International Covenant of Civil and Political Rights* — be immediately repealed, and that principles of humanity be observed in the treatment of all those held in detention, and in the implementation of all remaining emergency regulations and of the general law.

Returning to the process of negotiation it is suggested that a useful approach to take would be to clarify what is in the long-term interests of both the Tamil and Sinhalese communities. The natural tendency when faced with problems such as those requiring solution in Sri Lanka today, is to assume that unpleasant concessions are required by both sides, and that the only resolution, if indeed one is possible at all, will be a compromise which can satisfy no-one and leave all parties feeling aggrieved, feeling that they have given too much ground. In such circumstances the situation is still open to a renewal of the tensions and hostilities.

Negotiation is not necessarily synonymous with unpleasant concession, it can result in the discovery of common aims and aspirations. It is likely that, in the final analysis, the real aims of both groups — for economic prosperity, for democratic rights and for expression of humanitarian values — are not so very far apart.

This surely must be the basis of an effective and permanent resolution.

EPILOGUE

(October 8, 1987)

On July 29 1987 the Indo-Sri Lanka Accord was signed in Colombo by the President of Sri Lanka, Mr. Junius R. Jayawardene, and the Prime Minister of India, Mr. Rajiv Ghandi. The agreement to this Accord took most political observers and many of the people of Sri Lanka by surprise.

Its full text is reproduced after this section. Some of its important provisions include:

a provision that henceforth the official languages of Sri Lanka shall be Tamil and English as well as Sinhala;

the formation (until a referendum is held to ascertain the wishes of the inhabitants of the eastern province) of one administrative unit for the northern and eastern provinces;

provision for emergency rule to be lifted, for immediate cessation of hostilities and for the surrender of arms by the militants;

provision for a general amnesty to be extended to those held under the Prevention of Terrorism Act and other emergency legislation;

provision that the government make special efforts to rehabilitate into the mainstream of national life young Tamil militants and

provision for the government of India to underwrite and to guarantee these resolutions, and to co-operate in their implementation, and for the Sri Lankan government to request in this regard, as it has done, Indian military assistance.

With the concluding of this agreement the President of Sri Lanka has taken a bold step towards the restoration of order and harmony to his country. Whether the Accord will fulfil the aspirations hoped for it and achieve the aim of securing lasting peace is, of course, dependent on its thorough and successful implementation. Further, a good deal of work yet needs to be done if its full acceptance by the Sri Lankan community is to be won. Since the Accord represents a political compromise finally agreed to after much reluctance and conflict, it is perhaps not surprising that there is discontent with, and criticism of, some of its terms.

Indeed this discontent was made clear immediately. In the south there have been demonstrations, some peaceful and some violent. Clear protests have been made by members of the Buddhist clergy, prominent members of the government party, the SLFP, other parties and groups, and by some Sinhalese citizens. Government politicians have been attacked and in some instances killed. Perhaps most shocking was a grenade thrown in a cabinet meeting room in the well guarded Parliament building narrowly missing the President, killing one MP and injuring approximately 20 others.

It is reported that, as Tamil militants have been released under the agreement from detention camps in the south, those same camps have received Sinhalese detainees — persons suspected of fomenting unrest and anti-government activities.

Further, all has not proceeded peaceably in the north and east. Members of Tamil militant groups have failed to hand over all their arms as required by the Accord and have fought bitterly among themselves, causing considerable loss of life and physical injury. On October 5 the LTTE shot 8 captured Sri Lankan soldiers, apparently in retaliation for the suicide, earlier on the same day, of 12 Tamil militants being held in Sri Lankan government custody. Recently, in the eastern province Tamil militants are reported to have attacked and killed over 100 Sinhalese civilians.

If the Accord is to be allowed to succeed all factions must put the interests of peace and security in the country at the forefront of their consideration, and not allow, as has happened all too often in the past, short-term factional interests to prejudice the common good.

Undoubtedly there are many challenges ahead. In meeting those challenges it will be essential for the government, while legitimately expecting other groups to act with restraint, to face the fact that the violence which has erupted in the course of this protest may not be attributable to the Accord alone. It is possible that some of the unrest may reflect an underlying resentment felt by many Sri Lankan citizens at factors, outlined in earlier sections of this text, which contribute to certain undemocratic aspects of the present governmental system. These aspects — such as the failure to hold a general election when it was due, government conduct during the 1982 referendum, heavy press and media censorship and control, interference with the independence of the judiciary, and intolerance of peaceful protest and of dissent are issues which to some extent have been overshadowed by the communal violence. If consensus and harmony are to be regained it will be essential to confront and to deal with matters such as these.

One very real danger at present is caused by the serious security difficulties posed by malcontents bent on using violent means to make their views known. It is important that the government does take firm measures here. It is important also that, when fulfilling its mandate to maintain law and order, the government (or the Indian military forces should they intervene) take only those measures which are essential to this end, and avoid repeating a pattern which has occurred in the past

— of indiscriminate and arbitrary arrests, unnecessarily lengthy detentions, and abuses of power by police and military personnel.

For all the controversy that it has aroused the Accord undoubtedly is the most encouraging development which has occurred in Sri Lanka in recent times, providing, as it does, a framework for a solution to the ethnic violence. Here, to quote its words, is a real opportunity for Sri Lanka to become "a plural society in which all citizens can live in equality, safety and harmony".

If this does not work, what can? Its failure can result only in a return to violent communal strife, with all the tragedy and suffering that implies and with no hope left for a negotiated settlement. For these reasons it is vital that this opportunity for peace which the Accord does offer be realised and that its aims be brought to fruition.

THE INDO-SRI LANKA ACCORD

Sri Lanka Agreement

To Establish Peace and Normalcy in Sri Lanka

The President of the Democratic Socialist Republic of Sri Lanka, his excellency Mr. J.R. Jayewardene, and the Prime Minister of The Republic of India, His Excellency Mr. Rajiv Gandhi, having met at Colombo on July 29, 1987.

Attaching utmost importance to nurturing, intensifying and strengthening the traditional friendship of Sri Lanka and India, and acknowledging the imperative need of resolving the ethnic problem of Sri Lanka, and the consequent violence, and for the safety, well-being and prosperity of people belonging to all communities in Sri Lanka.

Have this day entered into the following agreement to fulfil this objective

in this context,

1.1 Desiring to preserve the unity, sovereignty and territorial integrity of Sri Lanka:

1.2 Acknowledging that Sri Lanka is a "multi-ethnic and a multi-lingual plural society" consisting, inter alia, of Sinhalese, Tamils, Muslims (Moors) and Burghers:

1.3 Recognising that each ethnic group has a distinct cultural and linguistic identity which has to be carefully nurtured:

1.4 Also recognising that the northern and the eastern provinces have been areas of historical habitation of Sri Lankan Tamil speaking peoples, who have at all times hitherto lived together in this territory with other ethnic groups:

1.5 Conscious of the necessity of strengthening the forces contributing to the unity, sovereignty and territorial integrity of Sri Lanka, and preserving its character as a multi-ethnic, multi-lingual and multi-religious plural society in which all citizens can live in equality, safety and harmony, and prosper and fulfil their aspirations:

2. Resolve that:

2.1 Since the Government of Sri Lanka proposes to permit adjoining provinces to join to form one administrative unit and also by a referendum to separate as may be permitted to the northern and eastern provinces as outlined below:

2.2 During the period, which shall be considered an interim period (i.e. from the date of the elections to the provincial council, as specified in para 2.8 to the date of the referendum as specified in para 2.3), the northern and eastern provinces as now constituted, will form one administrative unit, having one elected provincial council. Such a unit will have one governor, one chief minister and one board of ministers.

2.3 There will be a referendum on or before 31st december, 1988 to enable the people of the eastern province to decide whether:

a) The eastern province should remain linked with the northern province as one administrative unit, and continue to be governed together with the northern province as specified in para 2.2 or:

b) The eastern province should constitute a separate administrative unit having its own distinct provincial council with a separate governor, chief minister and board of ministers.

The President may, at his discretion, decide to postpone such a referendum.

2.4 All persons who have been displaced due to ethnic violence or other reasons, will have the right to vote in such a referendum. Necessary conditions to enable them to return to areas from where they were displaced will be created.

2.5 The referendum, when held, will be monitored by a committee headed by the Chief Justice, a member appointed by the President, nominated by the Government of Sri Lanka, and a member appointed by the President, nominated by the representatives of the Tamil speaking people of the eastern province.

2.6 A simple majority will be sufficient to determine the result of the referendum.

2.7 Meetings and other forms of propaganda, permissible within the laws of the country, will be allowed before the referendum.

2.8 Elections to provincial councils will be held within the next three months, in any event before 31st December 1987. Indian observers will be invited for elections to the provincial council of the north and east.

2.9 The emergency will be lifted in the eastern and northern provinces by August 15, 1987. A cessation of hostilities will come into effect all over the island within 48 hours of the signing of this agreement. All arms presently held by militant groups will be surrendered in accordance with an agreed procedure to authorities to be designated by the government of Sri Lanka.

Consequent to the cessation of hostilities and the surrender of arms by militant groups, the army and other security personnel will be confined to barracks in camps as on 25 May 1987. The process of surrendering of arms and the confining of security personnel moving back to barracks shall be completed within 72 hours of the cessation of hostilities coming into effect.

2.10 The Government of Sri Lanka will utilise for the purpose of law enforcement and maintenance of security in the northern and eastern provinces same organisations and mechanisms of government as are used in the rest of the country.

2.11 The President of Sri Lanka will grant a general amnesty to political and other prisoners now held in custody under the Prevention of Terrorism Act and other emergency laws, and to combatants, as well as to those persons accused, charged and/or convicted under these laws. The Government of Sri Lanka will make special efforts to rehabilitate militant youth with a view to bringing them back into the mainstream of national life. India will co-operate in the process.

2.12 The Government of Sri Lanka will accept and abide by the above provisions and expect all others to do likewise.

2.13 If the framework for the resolutions is accepted, the Government of Sri Lanka will implement the relevant proposals forthwith.

2.14 The Government of India will underwrite and guarantee the resolutions, and co-operate in the implementation of these proposals.

2.15 These proposals are conditional to an acceptance of the proposals negotiated from 4.5.1986 to 19.12.1986. Residual matters not finalised during the above negotiations shall be resolved between India and Sri Lanka within a period of six weeks of signing this agreement. These proposals are also conditional to the Government of India co-operating directly with the Government of Sri Lanka in their implementation.

2.16 These proposals are also conditional to the Government of India taking the following actions if any militant groups operating in Sri Lanka do not accept this framework of proposals for a settlement, namely,

a) India will take all necessary steps to ensure that Indian territory is not used for activities prejudicial to the unity, integrity and security of Sri Lanka.

b) the Indian navy/coast guard will co-operate with the Sri Lanka navy in preventing Tamil militant activities from affecting Sri Lanka.

c) In the event that the Government of Sri Lanka requests the Government of India to afford military assistance to implement these proposals the Government of India will co-operate by giving to the Government of Sri Lanka such military assistance as and when requested.

d) the Government of India will expedite repatriation from Sri Lanka of Indian citizens to India who are resident here, concurrently with the repatriation of Sri Lankan refugees from Tamil Nadu.

e) The Governments of Sri Lanka and India will co-operate in ensuring the physical security and safety of all communities inhabiting the northern and eastern provinces.

2.17 The Government of Sri Lanka shall ensure free, full and fair participation of voters from all communities in the northern and eastern provinces in electoral processes envisaged in this agreement. The Government of India will extend full co-operation to the Government of Sri Lanka in this regard.

2.18 The official language of Sri Lanka shall be Sinhala. Tamil and English will also be official languages.

3. This agreement and the annexure thereto shall come into force upon signature.

In witness whereof we have set our hands and seals hereunto.

Done in Colombo, Sri Lanka, on this the twenty-ninth day of July of the year one thousand nine hundred and eighty seven, in duplicate, both texts being equally authentic.

Junius Richard Jayewardene
President of the Democratic
Socialic Republic of Sri Lanka

Rajiv Gandhi
Prime Minister of the
Republic of India

ANNEXURE TO THE AGREEMENT

1. His Excellency the President of Sri Lanka and the Prime Minister of India agree that the referendum mentioned in paragraph 2 and its sub-paragraphs of the agreement will be observed by a representative of the election Commission of India to be invited by His Excellency the President of Sri Lanka.

2. Similarly, both heads of Government agree that the elections to the provincial council mentioned in paragraph 2.8 of the agreement will be observed and all para-military personnel will be withdrawn from the eastern and northern provinces with a view to creating conditions conducive to fair elections to the council.

The President, in his discretion, shall absorb such para-military forces, which came into being due to ethnic violence, into the regular security forces of Sri Lanka.

4. The President of Sri Lanka and the Prime Minister of India agree that the Tamil militants shall surrender their arms to authorities agreed upon to be designated by the President of Sri Lanka. The surrender shall take place in the presence of one senior representative each of the Sri Lanka Red Cross and the India Red Cross.

5. The President of Sri Lanka and the Prime Minister of India agree that a joint Indo-Sri Lankan observer group consisting of qualified representatives of the Government of Sri Lanka and the Government of India would monitor the cessation of hostilities from 31 July 1987.

6. The President of Sri Lanka and the Prime Minister of India also agree that in terms of paragraph 2.14 and paragraph 2.16 (c) of the agreement, an Indian peace keeping contingent may be invited by the President of Sri Lanka to guarantee and enforce the cessation of hostilities, if so required.

EXCHANGE OF LETTERS

President of Sri Lanka

July 29, 1987

Excellency,

Please refer to your letter dated the 29th of July 1987, which reads as follows:-

Excellency

1. Conscious of the friendship between our two countries stretching over two millenia and more, and recognising the importance of nurturing this traditional friendship, it is imperative that both Sri Lanka and India reaffirm the decision not to allow our respective territories to be used for activities prejudicial to each other's unity, territorial integrity and security.

2. In this spirit, you had, during the course of our discussion, agreed to meet some of India's concerns as follows:-

i) Your Excellency and myself will reach an early understanding about the relevance and employment of foreign military and intelligence personnel with a view to ensuring that such presences will not prejudice Indo-Sri Lanka relations.

ii) Trincomalee or any other ports in Sri Lanka will not be made available for military use by any country in a manner prejudicial to India's interests.

iii) The work of restoring and operating the Trincomalee oil tank will be undertaken as a joint venture between India and Sri Lanka.

iv) Sri Lanka's agreement with foreign broadcasting organisations will be reviewed to ensure that any facilities set up by them in Sri Lanka are used solely as public broadcasting facilities and not for any military or intelligence purposes.

3. In the same spirit, India will:

i) Deport all Sri Lankan citizens who are found to be engaging in terrorist activities or advocating separatism or secessionism.

ii) provide training facilities and military supplies for Sri Lankan security forces.

4. India and Sri Lanka have agreed to set up a joint consultative mechanism to continuously review matters of common concern in the light of the objectives stated in para 1 and specifically to monitor the implementation of other matters contained in this letter.

5. Kindly confirm, Excellency, that the above correctly sets out the agreement reached between us.

Please accept, Excellency, the assurances of my highest consideration.

yours sincerely

(Rajiv Gandhi)

His Excellency,

Mr. J.R. Jayewardene,

President of the Democratic Socialist Republic of Sri Lanka.,

Colombo

This is to confirm that the above correctly sets out the understanding reached between us.

Please accept, excellency, the assurances of my highest consideration

(J.R. Jayewardene)

President

LAWASIA

**The Law Association for Asia and the Western Pacific, 170, Phillip St.,
Sydney, NSW 2000, Australia. Cables "Lawasia" Telephone 221 2970**

LAWASIA is an association of lawyers — private lawyers, government lawyers, judges and law teachers.

LAWASIA is purely professional. It is non-governmental and does not engage in political activities. It promotes mutual understanding and friendship and co-operation to see that the law will best serve the peoples of the region.

LAWASIA is regional. Membership is restricted to Asia and the Pacific. Initially, membership is open to lawyers in countries which are members of ESCAP (the Economic and Social Commission for Asia and the Pacific). Other Asian and Pacific countries may be included by decision of the Council.

LAWASIA is controlled by the representatives of the member associations of practising lawyers in these countries. Such associations nominate the member for their country to the Council. Should more than one association in a country join, they jointly nominate the Councillor for that country.

LAWASIA was formed at a conference called by the Law Council of Australia in Canberra in August, 1966. Invitations were extended to the lawyers' associations of each country which was a member of the then ECAFE and representatives of eighteen countries attended.

LAWASIA's objectives include

● promoting the administration of justice, the protection of human rights and the maintenance of the rule of law
● advancing legal education
● diffusing knowledge of the laws of the member countries
● promoting development of the law, and uniformity where appropriate
● furthering international understanding and goodwill
● fostering relations and intercourse between lawyers in the region
● upholding and advancing the status of the legal profession in the region

LAWASIA operates through research groups studying particular legal problems in the region, through different Committees, of which the Human Rights Standing Committee is one, by putting visiting lawyers in touch with lawyers in countries they visit, by organising conferences and seminars of members and by setting up local groups to work for its aims. It publishes a legal journal, a twice-yearly Human Rights Bulletin, a bi-monthly Human Rights Newsletter, and the results of its research projects.